Also in The Crafts Series from Little, Brown
Gerald Clow, General Editor

BLACK AND WHITE PHOTOGRAPHY
Henry Horenstein

LEATHERWORK
Benjamin Maleson

POTTERY
Cora Pucci

WOODWORK
Raphael Teller

CROCHET
Mary Tibbals Ventre

Forthcoming

STAINED GLASS
Barbara Frazier and Gerald Clow

OFF-LOOM WEAVING

Jokers Wild (2½' x 5') by Elfleda Russell.

Detailed references as to how this hanging developed along the general lines of the working process are found, with the relevant techniques and shaping principles, in Chapters II and III. A sketch of the structure of this weaving appears on page 56.
Photograph by Richard Harper

OFF-LOOM
WEAVING

A Basic Manual

ELFLEDA RUSSELL

Diagrams by Elfleda Russell

LITTLE, BROWN AND COMPANY
BOSTON – TORONTO

First Edition

T 04/75

LIBRARY OF CONGRESS CATALOGING IN PUBLICATION DATA

Russell, Elfleda.
  Off-loom and card weaving.

  (The Crafts series)
  1. Hand weaving. 2. Card weaving. 1. Title.
TT848.R86   746.1′4   74-23685
ISBN 0-316-76295-4
ISBN 0-316-76296-2 pbk.

Designed by Barbara Bell Pitnof

Published simultaneously in Canada by Little, Brown & Company (Canada) Limited
Printed in the United States of America

TO MOM AND DADDY

Thanks for most of the house

The Little, Brown Crafts Series is designed and published for the express purpose of giving the beginner — usually a person trained to use his head, not his hands — an idea of the basic techniques involved in a craft, as well as an understanding of the inner essence of that medium. Authors were sought who do not necessarily have a "name" but who thoroughly enjoy sharing their craft, and all their sensitivities to its unique nature, with the beginner. Their knowledge of their craft is vital, although it was realized from the start that one person can never teach all the techniques available.

The series helps the beginner gain a sense of the spirit of the craft he chooses to explore, and gives him enough basic instruction to get him started. Emphasis is laid on creativity, as crafts today are freed from having to be functional; on process, rather than product, for in the making is the finding; and on human help, as well as technical help, as so many prior teaching tools have said only "how" and not "why." Finally, the authors have closed their books with as much information on "next steps" as they could lay their hands on, so that the beginner can continue to learn about the craft he or she has begun.

Gerald Clow

Acknowledgments

First, thanks to my many students of all ages whose spirited enjoyment of learning to weave is constant stimulation, and among whom this teacher is often student. Their continuing help and enthusiasm contributed immeasurably to this book, in a general way as well as specifically, since many of the works pictured are students' first pieces.

Special thanks to my design instructor, Penny Gouldstone, who, many years ago, first opened my eyes to design concerns and the fascination of fibers.

I must also thank our friends and associates in Boston and the New England area who, during our few years there, were the cause of many good things, of which the opportunity to do this book is one. To Gerry Clow my sincere appreciation for his support of my work. To the De Cordova Museum of Lincoln, Massachusetts, the Art Workshops of the Boston YWCA, and the numerous other craft organizations in the area must go recognition of the benefits to me of their support and furtherance of weaving as an art form.

To all those artists who responded to my request to represent their work, I am extremely grateful.

To Richard Harper goes my sincere appreciation for his patience, cooperation and skill in producing the fine photography that greatly enhances the publication.

Deepest gratitude goes to my family — to my parents for their help and encouragement through all the years, to my children, Christopher and Sabina, for being themselves and staying cheerful despite a year and a half of tripping over and losing their toys under mounds of paper — and to my husband Alan, for making my work possible by wanting our life to encompass my activities, and for providing help, counsel, and support wherever needed — from changing diapers, to running errands, to taking photographs, to editing, and doing all with equal finesse.

Contents

INTRODUCTION

Have you ever wanted to make your own wall hanging — sculpture — room divider — rug — elegant or outlandish clothing or body ornaments — interior decorating accessories — meditation chamber — or tie for your favorite streaker?

These can all be made with little more than your pair of hands, some yarn, and a sense of adventure. For the off-loom techniques are the various ways that threads can be intertwined without the need for any machinery, to offer a range of applications limited only by the imagination.

The basic off-loom techniques of finger weaving, macramé, twining, plaiting and card weaving are presented here. Along with these techniques are discussions of issues essential to being able to work out your own projects — which is, after all, where the fun begins. Issues like: where can ideas come from and what is actually involved in working them out off-loom? How can the off-loom techniques be applied to functional items? How do some weavers think who use this medium as an art form? And what concerns might you be facing if you decide to approach it from this point of view? . . . These are some of the points discussed in plain language that offer important clues to grabbing hold of your own creativity and getting over that hurdle of translating technical information into individual ideas.

All of the off-loom techniques, except card weaving, can be worked with free-hanging threads, allowing absolute freedom to shape — perhaps the single most striking quality of the medium. Although card weaving requires threads be stretched taut while they are worked, the lively patterned bands produced by merely passing threads through a pack of cards are quickly and easily woven with the same simplicity and directness characteristic of the other off-loom techniques. And it is shown here that the shaping principles used with free-hanging threads are capable of persuading even the traditionally straight card-woven strip to break out into shapes, too.

Although each of these techniques contains more than sufficient potential to be developed and used individually, their clear relationships to each other make the possibility of combining them too tempting to ignore. For the flexibility of the medium that allows threads to change direction freely and be added and subtracted also allows them to slip easily from one technique to another to produce rich changes of surface when forms are built with a combination of techniques.

The off-loom methods also place no restriction on the scale or type of materials that can be used, allowing a great variety of interpretation of their basic techniques. Indeed, each of the techniques and principles presented here can take on a completely different look when worked in the variety of fibers and cords that ranges from two-inch rope to fine linen through all the thicknesses and textures in between. Actually, any type of linear element is fair game for a restless imagination. Plastic tubing, electrical cord and used video tape are some of the unusual materials being explored in contemporary off-loom constructions.

Since the off-loom methods can be worked in virtually any situation, combining them with other media is a natural consequence of the freedom they allow. Off-loom techniques can be incorporated as easily into stitchery and the "soft" sculpture of stuffed fabric and plastic as they can be into rigid sculpture made with materials like wood, ceramic, Plexiglas and papier-mâché. They can also build onto found objects, such as driftwood, shoes, old computers, old TV sets, and scrap metal, when weavers choose to use the medium to accomplish gleefully some sort of transformation or rebirth of an article that has lived out its intended life.

This book begins with a suggested introductory exercise that details a way to explore the techniques and shaping principles that follow, to get acquainted with their natural qualities. The *off-loom working process* of Chapter I, and the discussion that precedes it, is the method I use to introduce students to the nature of working off-loom, that shows them how to get the most out of the medium — and themselves. Experiencing the working process can be a great aid in later planning and working out projects, for it points out possibilities for, and provides a perspective on, the information that follows.

Chapter II presents the free-hanging, off-loom techniques, and Chapter III presents methods of shaping them into forms. These shaping principles are actually building blocks that can be used to coax the free-hanging techniques to carry out your ideas and that can also be looked on as a positive source of ideas.

Chapter IV presents an extended study of card weaving — an ancient technique enjoying a recent surge of popularity. It is shown here that the potential of this very decorative and very useful technique is greatly expanded when shaping ideas borrowed from Chapter III are applied, along with implications transposed from other weaving methods. The message, of course, is that this is the means by which you can, if you wish, go on to develop the techniques of Chapter II even beyond what is pictured and described for them there.

Chapter V offers both inspiration and examples of further possibilities for off-loom and card weaving. Examples are studied for the role of idea, and the accompanying comments of some of the contributing artists provide the student of off-loom with an unusual opportunity to see right into some of the thinking that has led to several highly original applications of the medium.

The book is laid out for those who decide to use the off-loom working process as a means by which to explore the material that follows it. However, it's quite possible to work from the back to the front if some of the examples pictured there spark your plan of attack; or to work from the middle out, starting with some practice on the working board pictured at the beginning of Chapter II. So however you begin, happy weaving!

4

I

AN OFF-LOOM WORKING PROCESS

A Suggested Introductory Exercise

As described in the introduction, this chapter contains the method I use to introduce students to the nature of working with the qualities unique to off-loom. The aim is to show how the medium can be a tool in carrying out ideas as well as a source of ideas. The off-loom working process outlines a first way to practice the technical information that follows in a manner that challenges the beginner to deal with the basic kinds of decision every weaver faces in orchestrating individual projects.

What Is Involved in Learning to Construct Off-Loom

The most important concept to fix in your mind as you start your study of off-loom is the fact that learning to construct off-loom is actually learning to *integrate* the four distinct, but interdependent, factors that are the essential elements of any medium. These are: techniques, materials, design principles, and your individual personality. Learning to weave is actually learning to understand and control the impact of the last factor on the first three, as they in turn bounce off each other.

The Four Essential Elements
Feed Off Each Other

As you gain familiarity with a medium, each of these factors is capable of — and important in — stimulating and developing the other three. Your first work with off-loom would cheat you if it didn't provide you with an awareness of how these elements do feed off each other and start to build their own momentum — when you give them the chance by chipping away at all of them at once. It is this momentum that will enable you to become quickly independent in your pursuit of weaving ideas.

The Working Process Stimulates
the Simultaneous Development
of the Four Factors

A summary of the off-loom working process that follows reveals how it attempts to stimulate your awareness of the interdependence of these four factors and tries to help you develop all four together.

It begins by directing you to select only a few of the following techniques and shaping principles and materials to work with first. That selection should be based simply on preference as you examine the qualities and possibilities described and pictured with each. Next, you are guided through different stages of design concerns as you start practicing and manipulating the combination selected. Finally, on the basis of criteria set by you — hence, acting on personal preference again — you are encouraged to search gradually for a final form or idea in what develops through all this. What you learn about the medium in the first stages is harnessed in the last stage as you attempt to draw out, strengthen, and control a gradually forming idea. And as you work, your focus constantly shifts from exploring techniques and materials — to making design decisions — to exercising personal choice (the best way to understand how your individual nature can affect your use of off-loom) — and full circle back again, never staying too long with one before seeing how developments in the others can generate new possibilities for it.

Look for Ideas in Your Work, Listen to What the Medium Has to Say

A second goal just implied in the description of the integrative nature of the process is that it demonstrates how ideas can grow out of the very act of working threads. Encouraging you to begin this way, with an exercise where you discover the final form and idea through the gradual exploration, orchestration, and consolidation of a few techniques and shaping principles, is meant in part to point out a fruitful source of ideas for those who claim to have none. It also intends to suggest that the most beneficial way to begin with a new medium is in a manner that keeps you wide open to all that the medium can tell you about itself. This openness is important if you are going to learn to work *with* the natural tendencies of the medium, rather than unintentionally fighting them. The approach offered here, then, keeps you open and alert to the medium's message as long as possible, since being able to pull off your idea at the end depends on what you have learned of its nature in the meantime.

Different Relationships of Idea to Process

Chapter V offers the reverse of this relationship of idea to process by showing various ways by which ideas that stem from personal philosophy and day-to-day experience and, therefore, precede the made object, can feed *into* and affect the process of making it. Most methods of working involve some combination of idea feeding both in and out of the act of creating. The discussion of working through a series, and changing strategies, that comes after the end of the working process may provide some insight into how the relationship of idea to working process may adjust itself through different periods of work.

Selectivity and Looking in Depth

Selectivity is one of the few phenomena that one can safely say is involved in any design process. Outlining possible approaches to adopt for this important first step in your work is a basic message of the working process and the variations that follow.

Making any art or craft object must always involve selecting only some elements to work with from all the possibilities that exist. The nature of one's selection eventually becomes a prominent feature in fingerprinting one's work. The individualistic and innovative work of prominent artists is frequently directly linked with the nature of the limitations they set themselves and with their ability to convey surprising new insights as they demonstrate that expression for those limited means is still not exhausted after perhaps years of exploring them.

On every level, selectivity deserves careful consideration. For being able to work out projects depends on an ability to perceive the potential of elements, and that perception can be cultivated and developed by adopting in your own study of the medium the depth-versus-breadth focus just described.

When the working process directs you to select, then to stretch, by combining and making variations, it shows you a way of fully exploring materials, techniques, and shaping principles that stretches your own imaginative potential at the same time. You are encouraged to accumulate technical information at a rate that allows assimilation, synthesis, involvement of all the senses. Weaving well is not a matter of how much you know, it's a matter of what you *do* with what you know. Concentrate on pushing one set of off-loom elements as far as you can before moving on to a similar in-depth study of another set of techniques, shaping principles, and materials.

The Working Process Incorporates Answers to Beginners' Questions

Finally, answers to some fundamental questions brought up again and again by beginning students I have taught have also been incorporated into the process structure. Reading through it first — whether you adopt its procedure or just tuck some of its thoughts into your back pocket as you venture into your own method of exploring the technical information that follows — can help you prepare for situations that are bound to arise as you begin working threads.

A list of the headings discussed in the off-loom working process gives an idea of what is involved.

Working Process Headings

Choose a starting method and arrange to hang working strings

Select working strings

Chain a skeleton line: an optional beginning

Cut and mount working strings

Select the techniques and shaping principles to use in your first project

Introduce your elements by starting to practice the techniques and shaping
 — start fast
 — set clusters of working strings on collision courses
 — employ repetition with variation
 — leave doors open

Stop and look, build step upon step, join and divide again
 — methods of transition useful in integrating
 — control of color movement: active and passive threads
 — the key to controlling color movement
 — making working strings trade roles

Gradually replace concentration on varying detail with concern for the overall

— establish dominance

— search for and develop an overall form, an abstract idea, and/or an image

An Off-Loom Working Process

*Choose a Starting Method and Arrange to
Hang Working Strings*

However you begin should allow you maximum freedom to explore the flexibility of off-loom threads, so I suggest you get working strings hanging up, either against the wall or out in the middle of the room. The directions given here are for the simplest method of starting from a dowel; however, they could be adapted to either of the two sculptural starts presented in Chapter III — that of starting from a wire ring (pages 71 to 80) or starting from *spirals* or *cylinders* (particularly the *indirect cylinder*), discussed on pages 65 to 71. *Card weaving* would perhaps be better explored after the more immediate freedom allowed with the free-hanging techniques has been experienced. It will be apparent that the general nature of the process can be applied again and again to these and the many other starting methods suggested throughout the book.

Diagram 1 (page 14) pictures the starting procedure recommended here. A two-foot length (approximately) of half-inch dowel is hung on the wall by ataching a hanging cord two inches in from either end. Tack the cord at these points, or pass it through drilled holes and knot it below. This hanging cord can later be integrated into the work, so use yarn selected for the exercise.

Select Working Strings

Illustration 1 (page 13) pictures some of the yarns and cords used by weavers. You can see at a glance their different thicknesses and textures, and the different ways they hang. It's obvious that the native quality of whatever cords are chosen will strongly affect the character of what develops. Eventually you should try to experience handling a range of materials, to discover their different effects on the look of techniques and to

I-1. *Fibers and cords*

Left to right: 1. Unspun flax (fiber is two and a half feet long and strong). 2. Five-ply flax (like coarse linen). 3. and 4. Fine linen. 5. Heavy black and white twist; handspun on "Indian-type" spinning wheel with black alpaca and white mohair roving fed in simultaneously. 6. Heavy black handspun alpaca. 7. Heavy white handspun mohair. 8. Kinky thick and thin overspun wool, dyed with onion skins. 9. Hank of washed (purposely slightly matted) gray fleece to be weft that hangs out. 10. and 11. Metallic gold ribbons. 12. Tazlan — a commercial synthetic. 13. Variegated kinky acrylic. 14. Thick and thin white rayon. 15., 16., and 17. Slub rayons (irregular thickness). 18. Chenille. 19. Thick space-dyed chenille. 20. Glossy, novelty "balony." 21. Thick, dark, soft cotton. 22. Three-ply wool rug yarn. 23. Scandinavian Rya rug yarn (twisted and glossy). 24. Industrial acrylic roving (dyed). 25. Mariner's cotton seine twine (hard twist). 26. Sisal rope (springy). 27. Five-ply jute rope. 28. Thick jute roving. 29. Braided cotton oil-lamp wicking.

find which you prefer. Some of the novel materials pictured in Chapter V may be tried, too.

The selection of materials is such a personal thing that I hesitate to recommend any over others. The only reason to single out any now is for the sake of having you begin with threads that are easy to locate, easy to work with, and that show the techniques very clearly. For these reasons, then, I suggest using any medium-weight, nontextured cords. Appropriate ones pictured in Illustration 1 would be the five-ply flax at 2 (this is similar to coarse linen or medium-weight jute), the three-ply rug yarn at 22, and the cotton seine twine at 25. I usually have students work with three-ply rug yarn, which is about an eighth of an inch thick, because it is easily available in a range of colors. Wool, acrylic, and cotton rug yarn all work well. Check the source list for a number of suppliers. If you are eager to get going, just get heavy strings from your local hardware store, or even knitting worsted from the five-and-dime. Tightly twisted cotton seine twine is usually carried by local shops and has more body and spring than knitting worsted, but is generally limited to white, red, and green. A combination of seine

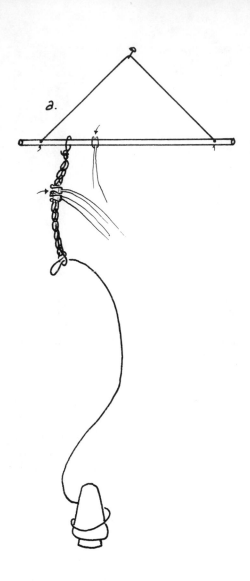

D-1. *A way to begin: chaining a skeleton line and starting to fill out the flesh*

twine and knitting worsted would work well and is easy to locate.

Work with three or four colors at most — and some of these could be shades of one color. An option would be to work with one color only, and focus attention on the forms and surfaces you achieve. Consider selecting colors with varied tones, ranging from dark to medium to light. Get approximately eight ounces of your favorite color, and four ounces each of the remaining ones.

Chain a Skeleton Line

Looking again at Diagram 1, you can see that the next step of starting from the dowel is to build what I term a "skeleton" above and below the dowel. As shown at the left, a chained line can feed out of one or more of your selected yarns, or it could be made of a much heavier, contrasting cord like jute rope, which could be covered later. The line wanders back and forth through itself, catching onto the dowel periodically and possibly looping up over the hanging nail. The skeleton thus built provides a base for your working strings to start from. As suggested in the diagram, mounting clusters of working strings at various points on both the rod and skeleton provides multiple starting points from which to begin practicing the off-loom techniques and shaping principles. As you gradually apply the "flesh," or solid masses of weaving, twining or knotting, a variety of situations must be coped with. Areas colliding, and the natural fall of the threads as they project at different angles, suggest of themselves shaping methods and textures, and maybe even new techniques that wouldn't be discovered otherwise.

Making the line of the skeleton is the fiber equivalent of *taking a line for a walk,* an exercise familiar to drawing students who are studying the changing qualities of line. As you build the line following the procedure described with Diagram 2 (page 16), think of varying the curves of the line and the sizes of the sections it cuts out when it passes through itself. Strive for a variety of scale with each.

Diagram 3 (page 17) shows the method of catching the skeleton onto the dowel when it needs that support or is to continue above.

The purpose of chaining this line, rather than just draping a

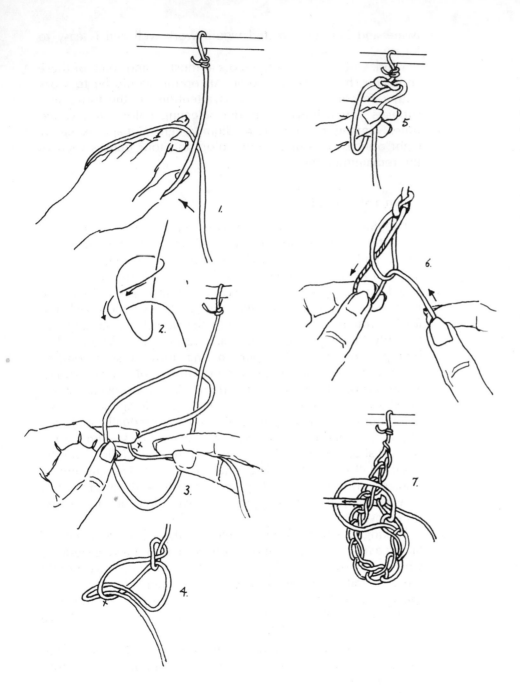

D-2. *Hand chaining the skeleton line*

1. Tie the end of a ball or cone of yarn to the dowel. Loop the yarn around your left hand just under to the left, then back over to the right, so the feeding length passes *behind* the tied end.

2. Push a length of feeding thread through this loop from right to left, as shown in 3.

3. When passing the second loop through the first, note how four fingers of the left hand are working. As this first complete link is tightened, adjust it up to the top of the string, by pulling back on the new loop at X.

4. The feeder will repeat the motion of step 3, passing through the second loop X.

5. The new position of the left fingers as they pull through all the loops after the first is shown where the second link starts the motion described at 4.

6. The chaining continues with a rapid seesaw motion. First, the *left* hand pulls down on the part of the loop shown striped to tighten that link, pulling the right hand up. Second, the *right* hand pulls down on the feeder until the loop tightens round the three fingers of the left hand, shown at 5. These fingers then grasp the feeder near where it exits from the last link and again pull down. Repeat.

7. A crochet hook can pass through any link of the chain to pull the feeder loop through that old link, as well as the working loop, thus catching the chain back through itself to outline a shape.

D-3. *Trapping the dowel (or other object) within the chain*

When it's time for the skeleton line to hook back onto the dowel for support, or to continue above it, trap the dowel (or any other object, as in Diagram 4) within a link of the chain by taking the loop that emerges from the chain (X) behind the dowel and passing the feeder loop (F) from in front of the dowel then through loop X as usual. Continue on as before.

I-2. *Exploring an alternative starting method, by Mary Anne Brodie*

A shaped spiral was the starting point for this student's experiment with a variation of the working process. Notice that some threads are proceeding upward to a second dowel and that others are knotting onto a wire holding cord being incorporated to produce rigid curves.

heavy rope, is that you will feel yourself building the line inch by inch, and it hooks through itself easily to outline areas.

If you are having difficulty getting the line started, listening to some favorite music, with the idea of interpreting its rhythm and mood in the proportions and movement of your chained line, may help you over the hurdle of beginning.

Don't panic if the network that develops appears chaotic — and you can't tell where it's heading. The skeleton does not have to suggest the final form. It's only there to get you concerned with a total from the start. Ninety percent of the skeleton may get chopped away in the process of the work. The chaos it suggests now can be the needed springboard that propels you to work — either to bring a sense of order out of it, to establish a relationship of dominance and subordination among all its parts, or even to bring out an image you eventually discover lurking there.

The skeleton is introduced, then, as something for you to put your attention to — to build onto or do battle with — in either case, a starting point for the forms to take off from.

In future experiments, the skeleton line may be played up or down or it may be eliminated entirely. Illustration 2 (below)

Alan Russell

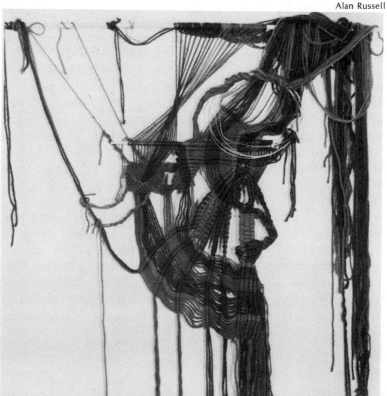

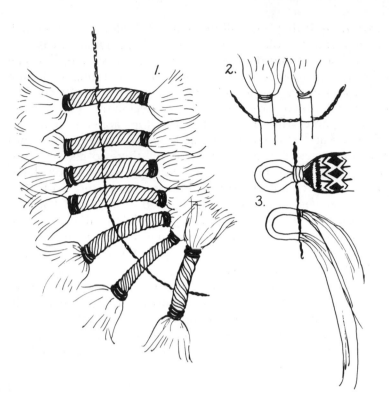

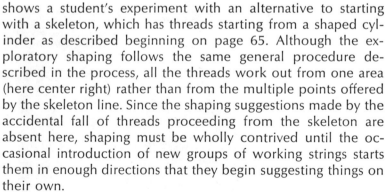

shows a student's experiment with an alternative to starting with a skeleton, which has threads starting from a shaped cylinder as described beginning on page 65. Although the exploratory shaping follows the same general procedure described in the process, all the threads work out from one area (here center right) rather than from the multiple points offered by the skeleton line. Since the shaping suggestions made by the accidental fall of threads proceeding from the skeleton are absent here, shaping must be wholly contrived until the occasional introduction of new groups of working strings starts them in enough directions that they begin suggesting things on their own.

Diagram 4 (above) pictures other uses of the chained line that can be explored later. Here, prepared off-loom elements are caught into the growing chain to give the process a very structured beginning. Spacing can be orchestrated as the chain builds, and the chain can be left as is or later wrapped or knotted over. Very little shaping of the tails may be needed to complete a piece started this way.

D-4. *Other uses for the chain*

1. and 2. A frayed rope ladder is made when a series of wrapped, frayed sections of thick sisal are caught into the chain. Any repeated elements could be incorporated this way, whether they are found objects like bones, or made elements like these.
3. The looped and wrapped ends of a band of card weaving are caught into the chain, as are a bundle of working strings.
4. The two upper elements are quickly prepared by stringing cards, as shown for the two-color weave in Chapter IV, and spacing out two five-inch sections of weaving, wrapping the skipped warp length between. Long, released warps coming from either end can be intertwined in some manner after the pieces are assembled.

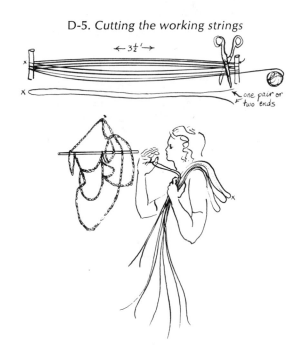

D-5. *Cutting the working strings*

← 3½' →

x

x

one pair or two ends

Cut and Mount Working Strings

Diagram 5 (left) shows an easy way to prepare working strings. Find a place where you can wind off a three-and-a-half-foot-long (minimum) loop of working strings. The end of a kitchen table or between chairs can work. To start, make at least eight complete circles with a color you select to be dominant, and four circles each of the remaining colors. You will be winding off many more working strings as work develops.

Cut the loops only at the end of the loop where you started winding, and from four circles you will have four looped pairs or eight individual working strings. (See the one pair pictured here.)

Toss the loops over your left shoulder, and clutching them with your left hand, pull out pairs by the loop — and no tangles! The looped ends (X) of your pairs of strings are now mounted on the dowel and upper parts of the skeleton line, as suggested back in Diagram 1 (page 14), using the *reverse lark's head,* the first off-loom technique presented in Chapter II (page 35).

Mount these threads in a variety of groupings. Combine different colors and different quantities of threads to make groupings of anywhere from four threads to thirty-two threads per group. You will be continually adding more threads as work develops downward and upward and you apply more flesh to the skeleton. Eventually, hundreds of strings may be building one section.

Place the first groups of working strings in fairly close proximity so they can be joined to form larger areas before developing too far on their own, and begin practicing the techniques as described next. Making sections join, divide, and join up again differently can continue in variations throughout the process and be a major motivation for keeping it moving.

It should be mentioned now that winding up the ends of your working strings into "butterflies" is discouraged as it adds clutter that distracts from the important viewing of the fall of the threads out of completed work, which always precedes the next step. Learn to toss threads aside consistently as you use them, using a number of the type of paper clamps pictured in Diagram 11 (page 38) to clamp temporarily unused threads out of the way as you work. Release them to view the piece.

Even with ten-foot working strings, working them hanging and tossing them consistently makes tangling no problem.

*Select the Techniques and Shaping Principles to
Use in Your First Project*

Just two off-loom techniques and two or three shaping principles will provide more than enough variety to develop in one study. This same general process can be set in motion again later, using different combinations of techniques and shaping principles, different starting methods, and different project goals.

Select a combination that provides clear contrasts. One suggestion is *weaving* combined with the *double half hitch* (pages 37 to 42), both worked using the shaping principles of *walking to the left and right, accumulating,* and *fanning* (pages 59, 60, and 63). The importance of this selection in characterizing your work has already been mentioned, so, eventually, you should try different combinations that force you to grapple with different problems.

For now, contrast or just preference can guide your selection. The fact that most of the shaping principles are depicted with the suggested weaving and double half hitch combination will make their selection bypass the problem of translating shaping instructions into other techniques on the first try.

As soon as you can recognize the various off-loom techniques and methods of shaping, it will be worthwhile studying the examples of completed off-loom work presented in this and the final chapter to see what kind of selection occurred in each.

*Introduce Your Elements by Starting to Practice
the Techniques and Shaping*

Start fast. Study all the references here to those techniques and shaping principles you will be working with. Decide whether you want to study other weavers' applications of them, pictured here, before or after you try working them yourself.

Begin practicing your techniques and shaping principles on different groups of mounted threads. As soon as possible, practice each technique on a large enough grouping to get a good idea of its texture.

Quickly try out everything you can think of doing with your elements. Don't slow yourself down — or tie yourself down — with long-range plans at this point. This is the time to get acquainted with your stew — so introduce the elements with urgency and in necessarily arbitrary fashion. Get them sizzling up in front of you right away.

Set Clusters of Working Strings on Collision Courses. The main thing to calculate now is that groupings should soon start to follow shaping that will direct them onto *collision courses*. Forcing sections to join together, or flow through each other, or in some way respond to each other before developing too far independently makes you concentrate on the important design principle of *transition* — the flow or movement from one detail to another. A hazard of working off-loom is to neglect to unite the many small details that develop into a few large simple masses. Methods of joining isolated sections are discussed on pages 22 to 23 and pictured in Diagram 32 (page 63). These important sequence drawings should be looked at now, for they illustrate the gradual way threads build with the working process. Anyone having difficulty getting started could follow the sequence to begin, then take off and finish it independently. .

Employ Repetition with Variation. Realize that the selection of a limited means to work with is calculated to force you to repeat continually your elements. As you begin building sections that are aimed at each other, attempt to make some change every time you repeat a technique or shaping principle. The number of threads used, the density of the work, the direction the technique builds in, the arrangement of the colors, the fragmenting and redirecting of a much-used shaping principle — these are some basic methods of creating variations.

The following specific variations can be referred to when your own ideas run out.

— See what basic shapes result from your shaping principles.
— Change the scale and silhouette of these shapes by using different numbers of threads to complete them, and by joining them up with other sections at different points and in different ways.

— Interrupt one shaping principle with another, then return to the original.

— Have each color form large and small solid areas.

— Trap a small solid area of one color within a field of another. (Note the discussion of *active* and *passive* threads on pages 23 to 24 for the means to make colors appear and disappear to achieve entrapment.)

— Blend the colors in some areas by alternating the threads in different mixes, such as: aaa, bbb, aaa (three threads of each color alternating); a, b, a (one of each); a, bbb, a, bbb (three of one to every one of the other).

— Trap mixed color areas within solid ones and vice versa.

— Build an area using one technique and color, then pass a strip of the second color through, changing to another technique within that strip.

— Do the same thing again, this time not changing the technique.

— Make areas bulge out and cave in.

— Make areas push out sideways.

Leave Doors Open. Make a point of leaving some sections of unworked threads trapped at various locations within the continuing work. Return to weave, knot, or twine across these spaces toward the end, when you know what colors and treatment will best complement what has developed in the meantime. You will be glad to have kept these doors open when you are trying to pull everything together and to clarify dominance, contrast and transitions, which become major considerations in the later stages of working a piece.

Diagram 32 (page 63) pictures how to trap threads to be worked later. Reference to this technique is also made in the description of *Om* (page 77), since open doors were an important feature in the development of that piece.

Stop and Look, Build Step upon Step,
Join and Divide Again

Methods of Transition Useful in Integrating. Work continues by looking for the next step in the way threads emerge from the previous one. Keep stopping to see what you have so far. What lines of color have started to form? How can existing shapes be folded or bent over? How can they be continued on in the same direction or turned to change direction? Do you see links between different edges that you can develop?

Keep trying to join sections into much larger masses that provide a change of scale, then break them up again — but differently this time.

Again, looking at the series of drawings of Diagram 32, you will see how off-loom work can grow gradually, building, joining, dividing, repeating. Viewing elaborate finished work shouldn't make you forget that decisions are made essentially one at a time. Where they finally lead can be as much of a surprise to the maker as it is to the viewer.

Notice also in this diagram how smooth transitions are achieved by: first, pulling the movement of one section right into the mass it joins by continuing the first movement through a change of technique in the second mass (see B, page 62); second, starting a new section from a point that implies a continuation of a previous movement (see D, page 63); third, carrying an occasional line across several sections to tie them together (see J, page 63).

Notice also the variety of ways new threads are introduced at F, K, L and M.

Incorporating this sequence into your work, or as already mentioned, starting with it and using it as a jumping-off point, may clarify the transition principles that function here, so that you understand how to proceed yourself.

Control of Color Movement: Active and Passive Threads. As your different-colored working strings move through the techniques and shaping principles, you will notice certain movements of color occurring as a natural response to work performed. Directing the flow of color can help motivate your continuing manipulation of the working process, once certain relationships between technique and color position are understood.

First, notice in the off-loom techniques presented here that in performing most of the techniques, some threads remain passive while others do all the work — or are active. In the double half hitch (page 40) the *holding cord* is passive and the *knotters* are active. In the *half knot* (page 51), the two central strings are passive and the two outside knotting strings are active. In *wrapping* or *coiling* (page 46), the same situation has the central cord or cords passive, while the cord doing the coiling is active. In *twining* (page 43), the *warps* are passive while those strings doing the twining are active. In weaving (page 42), we usually think of the *weft* as active, the warps as passive.

But in weaving this isn't always necessarily the case, and in explaining why, I want to switch our active-passive classification from being in terms of how the threads act when they carry out the technique to how the threads appear in the completed technique.

Now we will say that the active threads are those we see when the technique is finished, while the passive threads are those we either don't see or else see less of. For all of the techniques listed above, except weaving, those threads that were active in making the technique are also the active or visible threads in the finished technique. Similarly, in each case except weaving, the threads that are passive in making the technique are also passive or hidden in the completed technique. The knotters, twiners, coilers are the threads, then, whose colors are seen; the holding cords, wrapped cords, twined warps are the threads whose colors are not seen.

In weaving, although the weft is usually active in making the weave, three different types of surfaces can appear in the end. Diagram 28 (page 61) shows the possibilities of having only the weft appear on the surface *(weft face weave),* only the warp appear *(warp face weave),* or having a mix of both the warps and the wefts appear. So, with respect to the appearance of weaving, we can have either the wefts *or* the warps active or a neutral situation where there is a blend, or equal appearance of both.

The Key to Controlling Color Movement. Since we see the colors of the active threads and don't see the passive threads, it becomes obvious that colors can be moved here and there at will by using the appropriate shaping principle and making whichever thread that you want to be seen through that section active in making its technique.

Making Working Strings Trade Roles. To get the most out of the limited selection of threads, techniques, and shaping principles chosen to be concentrated on in your first manipulation of the working process, try to make each thread act and appear both active and passive for each technique used, as they travel through your shaping. This is referred to as *trading roles*. And, whether or not weaving is selected to be one of the first off-loom techniques tried, take the hint from its neutral balanced weave that, besides appearing and disappearing, colors can also be mixed.

As the warps and wefts intertwine to present a mixed blend of colors in the balanced weave, so any surface you make with other techniques that break up the color to produce a spotted or striped area provides the third possibility of mixed colors. Diagram 14 (page 41) shows a dark and a light thread trading roles to be both active and passive in making the double half hitch, simply by changing from horizontal to vertical rows of hitches. It also shows the threads mixed within the balanced weave at *a*. Coarser color mixing can be achieved by alternating between vertical and horizontal double half hitches within a row, as shown at 2 of that drawing.

So the movement of a color can continue from one section through another, even if techniques change, as long as the color remains either active — to create a strong, solid color continuation — or mixed — to create a softer continuation.

It may help you to keep the working process going by concentrating on creating paths of color that continue across different sections, made with different techniques, to tie the smaller sections into a few simple, large movements. You might discover, and develop or emphasize, only certain movements of the many possible ones opened up in the necessarily random way the process has to start.

Gradually Replace Concentration on Varying Detail with Concern for the Overall

There will come a time when enough variety is introduced, and it's necessary to begin repeating or drawing attention to something you already have, so that all the forms and colors and surfaces don't exist in equal quantity and confuse the design.

Establish Dominance. There is often a thin line between a chaotic piece of off-loom work and one that holds together as a total unit. One basic compositional device that can help bring a sense of order to your work now is the establishment of *dom-*

inance and *subordination*. Making one color and/or one shape and/or one technique start to dominate the others by appearing more and more, perhaps in some highlighted fashion, makes the remaining elements recede to a subordinate state. This kind of emphasis can do much to save from confusion and chaos a piece containing a lot of variety.

Search for and Develop an Overall Form, an Abstract Idea, and/or an Image. Look hard at your work to find something to bring out in the final stages. Clarifying dominance may be enough. There are other things that can be considered as well, to seek out as motivation in the last stages. Anything about the work that appeals to you and seems possible as its final statement is valid. Don't hesitate to cut out or redo areas that now seem inappropriate.

Some may want to recognize a familiar image. If you see an elephant in your piece, by all means go ahead and make it into an elephant! Perhaps an appealing overall abstract form is emerging that requires a little more clarity. Maybe some symbolism will catch your eye, or a philosophical metaphor suggested by the conflict of forms.

Only you can decide what terms you want to think in at this point. If you draw a complete blank, study the works and artists' comments of Chapter V for ideas.

Footnotes

Objectively viewing your piece to make reasonable final decisions is sometimes next to impossible after being engrossed in a work over a period of time. Some tricks that can help you see it again are to: hide it away overnight or for a few days before making final decisions . . . view it in a mirror . . . squint to obliterate detail and detect overall forms and movements to emphasize . . . sketch alternative completions. I find that the feeling for the final form usually grows gradually through the development of the piece. There isn't always one precise moment when an idea hits. So stay flexible, but be on the lookout for big trends through much of the work.

The Working Process Summarized

Choose a way to start — begin rapidly and with abandon. Introduce and familiarize yourself with the off-loom techniques and shaping principles and the materials you have selected — build step upon step, looking for the next move in the last, employing repetition with variation. Gradually shift focus to the overall development. Look for simple forms, an idea, qualities to emphasize that grow out of the work itself.

Working Through a Series: How Strategies Change

The nature of the process just described keeps the weaver highly flexible to the end of the piece, so that as much information as possible can be absorbed from the act of working the threads, and so that ideas can be drawn out of the working experience.

If you carry on to do future pieces with some variations of the off-loom working process, or of an idea that grew out of it, you will be working in a *series* — a term used to describe the presence of some constant in a number of sequential works.

Working in a series is a way of pushing an idea to a greater degree of maturity, refinement, and certainly individualization, than occurs when work consists of a lot of one-shot efforts.

Individuals tend by their nature to prefer working either more "spontaneously" or according to prior plan. Whichever accent the personality places on the manner in which work is carried out, the general strategy tends to shift, along with the experience acquired through a developing series, from early strategies stressing spontaneity — taking the clues from the work — to later strategies characterized by an increasing degree of preconception — the ability and wish to establish more and more criteria before work commences.

This may mean simply that as you get further into a series, you come to plan certain vague aspects of the general form or movement or content of projects ahead of time. However, if the desire to preconceive pulls someone new to a medium too quickly out of the preliminary, flexible, exploratory stage, that student is prematurely shut off from all the yet unabsorbed information that the medium has to offer.

In other words, planning too early in the learning stage closes your eyes to opportunities and lessons offered by the continuing work. Discipline yourself not to be concerned at first about being able to use your first work, and don't be worried about not seeing how it's going to end up until the final stages. The longer you sustain flexibility, the more you will learn and have to work with later.

Those who intend to venture into a series will find use for the alternate working methods described below, and accompanying some of the individual techniques and shaping principles presented in Chapters II, III, and IV.

Other Exercises

The working process just detailed recommends the selection of three or four colors, two techniques, and three shaping principles, which you combine to evolve as much variety as you can. *Jokers Wild* (title page) roughly followed this selection and the stages of development described in the process. Diagram 25 (page 56) points out the main structural features of this piece.

The following list of exercises is designed to strengthen your sensitivity and imagination by limiting different elements and forcing different types of focus and expansion.

Use Many Shaping Principles, One Color, One Material, and One or Two Techniques

— Changes of form must produce most of the interest. Make dramatic, sudden, and severe changes of directtion. Narrow shapes in, make them pop out.
— Sculpt as varied forms as possible, thinking of "open" and "closed" shapes, or shapes that project outward versus those that are smooth-sided, self-contained, full.

Example: Cocoons (page 69). The description of how this piece developed may be useful in starting in with this approach.

*Use Many Techniques, Many Materials of Just One Color, and
One Shaping Principle*

— Concentrate on different surfaces coating a cluster of shapes that are clearly a "family" — variations on one form.

— Use different-textured materials and very contrasting techniques.

— Consider assembling a number of separately started, related forms. Completing them can glue them together.

Example: Assemble a number of spirals, cylinders, and cones into a sort of totem that contains as rich a variety of surfaces as you can come up with.

*Use Many Colors, One Technique, and
One or Two Shaping Principles*

— Concentrate on pulling the eye around the piece by creating paths of color that are "direct," or clearly and continuously drawn, and paths that are "indirect," or broken and implied. In other words, play with the movement of solid and dotted lines and areas. The control of active and passive threads and methods of transition can be concentrated on here.

Examples: The double half hitch or *double twining* would both be good techniques to use here. The result may be a sort of shaped tapestry. *Siamese Hat* (page 68) can be looked at as another interpretation of this exercise.

*Start with a Subject — a Realistic Image or Abstract
Concept — and Select Whichever Combination of Elements
Seems Appropriate*

Ideas drawn from nature, from casual experience, or from personal philosophy will likely be approached in this manner.

Example: Donkey (page 164), the work of Evelyn Roth (page 165), and Anita Fisk's *Albatross* (page 47) are a few of the many varied examples of this approach that can be found throughout the book.

Start from Some Materials or Objects That Particularly
Appeal to You and Let Them Suggest How a Piece Can Develop

There is great latitude for imagination here. A sensitivity to your environment and an eye for possibilities in the unexpected are personal qualities that can lead naturally to this approach.

Examples: Karen M. Van Derpool's *Emanon* (page 168), Shirley Fink's *American Primitive* (page 159), Mary Ventre's *Domes* (pages 160 and 161) all appear to have been stimulated to some degree by a response to the suggestion of materials.

Start a Cylindrical Sculpture or Light Fixture from Rings,
Employing Symmetry; Select Elements That Are Appropriate

A discussion of some of the advantages and hazards of working with symmetry accompany the description of *Om,* starting on page 71. A sculpture such as *Om* can become a dramatic light fixture if one light bulb, or a series of lights (perhaps colored), is carried down the center. The recent availability of *fiber optics,* a fine, flexible, fiberlike tube that can emit a spot of light at its open tip, means that handfuls of this remarkable material could be caught right into the developing fiber sculpture so that the sculpture itself is eventually plugged in to come to life with dancing spots of light.

Example: Om (pages 72 to 74).

Create a Piece of Clothing or a Body Ornament Using
Whatever Elements Serve Your Needs

Interpretation of this exercise could range through the following:

— a beautiful example of the traditional idea of a necklace;
— a front and back neckpiece that is seen coming and going — and grows downward as far as you want;
— a beautifully designed piece of traditional clothing, such as a vest, a belt, a poncho, a jacket, a skirt;
— a wild interpretation of what clothing actually is, which complements or negates the figure and may result in a bizarre body covering or costume. Ritualistic, primitive costumes could be studied for ideas.

— a lively costume that becomes a wall hanging when not being worn;

— and — how can I resist . . . an appropriately revealing ornament to be worn by a streaker.

Examples: *Siamese Hat,* by Francie Rosenblatt (page 68); the vest on page 80; Evelyn Roth's work on page 165; the clothing suggestions in Diagram 41 (page 86); the belts on pages 116 and 122.

Create a Spatial Environment for Some Purpose — Possibly to Provide Escape to Whatever You Consider Paradise, or to Act as a Meditation Chamber

The combination of heavy rope and armatures with traditional off-loom materials and whatever else adds to the poetry of your environment could produce a large or — if you prefer — intimate enclosure that stands in a corner of a room or outside, or that hangs, such as a womblike swing that you can climb into and relaxingly rock back and forth in. Making a piece crawl along the floor, bend to climb the wall, then come out along the ceiling and hang down would be one way to work with the existing interior: making a sort of rug, wall hanging and canopy, all in one.

As with the working process, these suggested exercises can be returned to after you practice the following off-loom techniques and shaping principles or can be a medium through which you practice them. In any case, Chapter I is intended to give you some insights into possibilities for what follows.

II

OFF-LOOM TECHNIQUES

The off-loom techniques that can be worked on free-hanging threads are presented here. Because of its special nature, card weaving is presented separately in Chapter IV and explored in depth to demonstrate the varied potential that reveals itself when you scratch below the surface of any technique. The value of Chapter IV then, beyond what is stated about that technique itself, is that it can stand as a model of how each of the techniques that follow now can also be expanded.

Encouraging you to apply the principles of shaping, outlined in Chapter III, to the techniques that follow now, as a method of developing their potential in your own way, is one of the main messages of this book. Always looking for the simple mechanism that makes a technique work is still another important step in developing its potential, for clues to what will alter its look are contained there. Some instances of both these development methods are cited with certain techniques to assist you in recognizing how to develop further variety with the techniques on your own.

Those who have decided to begin with the working process will be trying to decide which techniques to focus on first. Descriptions of applications and possibilities that accompany techniques will be of interest to them, as well as to those with some other specific project in mind.

Although I strongly recommend you begin practicing the free-hanging techniques on threads hanging down from a dowel that is attached to the wall, some who are just beginning may find it convenient to get some preliminary practice on a working board, set in your lap, propped against a table. A 12" x 18" piece of Bainbridge board, or even corrugated cardboard, serves well. Mounting threads on the board and working against it can be almost like having an extra pair of hands, which you will want at first, in that slits cut into the sides and bottom can hold threads taut on whatever angle is needed as you practice the weaving, knotting, and twining and methods of shaping that follow.

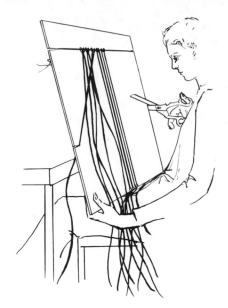

Here the weaver is preparing to practice a diagonal row of double half hitches — one of the most useful macramé knots — and the holding cord is held taut by the slit, leaving both hands free to make the knot, pictured in Diagram 13 (page 40). You may wish to perfect two or three techniques in this manner before moving to the wall. It is generally a good idea, though, to work a piece in the same situation as it is to be presented whenever possible. A wall hanging should be worked on the wall, a hanging sculpture can be worked suspended from the ceiling, a standing form can be worked on a table, the floor, in your lap. Only small, flat projects, such as belts, neckpieces, vests, cushions, are appropriately completed on a working board. Since the board is rather confining and may cause you to lock attention into small detail, set it aside after an hour or two and get those threads hanging.

D-7. *The reverse lark's head and the expanded reverse lark's head*

The looped end (X) of your pairs of working strings (see Diagram 5, page 19) can be mounted onto whatever device your threads work onto using the *reverse lark's head* (1 to 4) and, in some cases, the *expanded reverse lark's head* (6 and 7). The device mounted onto may be a dowel, a chained skeleton line, a wire ring, a string tied round a working board, a belt ring, a found object, a ceramic form . . . etc.

1. Pass the loop behind the dowel (or other object), then up over the top, and pull it down in front for about two inches.
2. Holding this loop in your left hand, pull its two tails forward through the loop with your right hand.
3. A completed reverse lark's head.
4. This knot mounts threads very densely, for both ends of each pair of working strings emerge from between the two mounting loops. This is useful for beginning areas of dense weaving. However, where you start into a more open weave or into areas of double half hitches (Diagram 13, page 40) — where each individual knotting string emerges from between its own two loops, thereby spacing working strings twice as wide apart as they are in this mounting — the first row of work will look neater if the mounting is expanded.

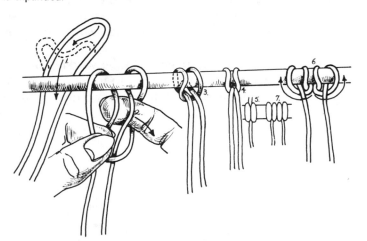

5. Diagram of a double half hitch, where each string makes two loops.
6. The expanded reverse lark's head: Widen the mounting to four loops by first making the simple knot then looping the left string over the dowel to the left and the right string over the dowel to the right. Make these hitches start in front then pass over the top and down behind the dowel, finishing by coming forward through their own loops. When you study the double half hitch diagram on page 40, you will notice that these expanding loops are actually half hitches.
7. This expanded reverse lark's head has every working string now emerging from between its own two loops, so the mounting now looks just like the double half hitch to its left.

Use this expanded knot both to begin areas of double half hitches and to introduce new strings into their midst.

D-8. Starting to weave, the warp and the weft

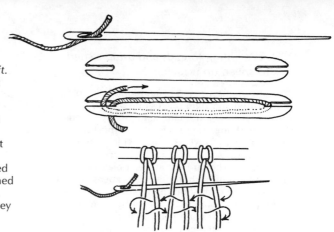

If you have ever darned socks you already know how to weave. In weaving terms, those threads that are first strung back and forth across the opening are *warps*, the thread carried in the needle that darns over and under the warps to fill in is the *weft*. Consider any group of at least eight mounted threads as a cluster of warps and start weaving under and over as shown. Notice that in the return row, the weft opposes the weave of the first row by starting back under the last warp it just wove over.

To carry the weft, get the largest needle you can find. Weaving and darning needles are available in three- and four-inch lengths.

It doesn't take long to realize that although the needle is handy for getting into tight places, it is a bother weaving big spaces, where a long tail of weft trails behind and has to be pulled all the way through at the end of each row. The shuttle pictured here can be purchased at any craft store or cut from Bainbridge cardboard (mentioned already as a useful working board). You will want a collection of at least three sizes, one four-inch, one six-inch, and one eight-inch. If you are making them yourself, they are usually about one and one half inches wide. Ambitious weavers can cut them from plywood veneer and sand and wax or shellac them for smooth sailing. The weft is wound onto the shuttle to start and is gradually let out as its length gets used up in the weaving.

D-9. Vary the lines of the weaving

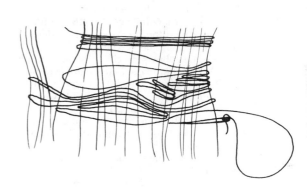

Don't make an effort to keep lines straight as you weave. You may want to start with a few straight rows of weaving, just to see what a horizontal stripe looks like. But soon start exploring different qualities of line by patting your weft lines into curves, using your fingers or a fork. See what variety of line you can make as wefts wander at will. Sometimes repeat sections of curve to build up rhythms. The edges of the work needn't be straight. Don't always weave all the way across. Reverse direction frequently, sometimes to build dense sections within the overall mass. At some point, continue a row of weaving farther on to include more warps at one side.

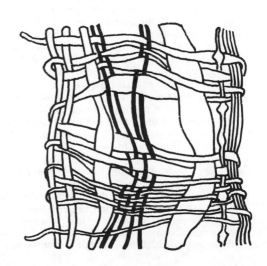

D-10. Vary the textures of the weave by changing the materials and the weaving sequence

As you play with the lines of weaving, begin introducing a few different yarns so you can observe the changes as various weights and textures of threads intertwine. Further, sometimes weave over and under several threads at once — say, over three under three for a while, then over three under one. You can begin inventing irregular textures and regular patterns with this process.

D-11. *Weighting threads and using a shed stick to speed up weaving*

This convenient method of temporarily keeping warps sorted and rigid makes one of every two woven rows automatic, and greatly speeds up your weaving. These devices are most useful where you plan to weave into a wide section of vertical warps.

1. The shuttle shown here at *a* is a plastic fisherman's netting shuttle, very inexpensive and available from craft shops and marine suppliers — ideal for off-loom work. Begin by clamping the widest paper clamp you can find, or series of clamps, onto the group of warps you will be weaving into, about one and a half feet down their length, as shown at *c*. Weave your shuttle from left to right. Before pulling it out at the right, turn it on edge to form a *shed,* shown at 1a, to be the opening between the front and back warps that the shuttle will pass through. Insert a ruler (or facsimile cut from Bainbridge cardboard), called the *shed stick,* just under the shuttle, where the shed is widest, and slide it down to sit just above the clamp, as shown at *b.* Then pull your shuttle out at the right, leaving the weft in that shed. Weave back from right to left, going under and over the opposite weave by hand as usual. You can push up the previous row with the shuttle before pulling it out. To weave row three and every future odd-numbered row that comes from the left, turn the shed stick on edge and pass the shuttle through the shed at the widest point. The left-hand row is the hardest for a right-handed weaver to darn by hand, so this process that makes it automatic very much speeds the weaving.

The solid outline at *b* shows the shed stick back vertical (at rest) while rows are woven by hand from right to left. The dotted outline shows it turned on edge to form the shed for the left to right rows, with the threads that are behind the stick pushed back (B) and the threads that are in front of it pushed forward (F). The sketch at 1a shows this clearly.

2. After completing a vertical section of weaving, try tying the clamp to the rod to curve the warps sideways. Other wefts can then be woven or knotted or twined through, to hold the warps in this position. This would be one way of immediately setting up and dealing with colliding clusters of threads, brought up in the working process (page 21), and elaborated on in the sequence drawings (page 63).

3. Remove the clamp and watch how the released warp ends fall. As they emerge here, they suggest drawing 4 — weaving down through themselves. Notice the triangular shape that results. Where could it go next to keep the exercise moving? The shaping principles in Diagram 26 (page 59) are actually variations on what is shown here. Notice how the warps themselves have turned to become temporary wefts. They have "changed roles" by doing this, and could change again to become knotters, holding cords, twining cords, or warps again. This is why it's best not to think of threads as warps or wefts when you are working off-loom. Just think of them as threads all having equal potential to play any role and to change that role at any time.

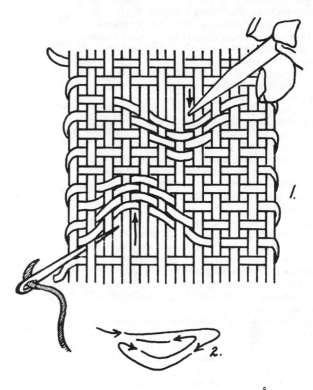

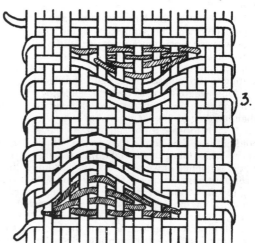

D-12. *Inlaid weaving*

1. Sections of plain weaving can be worked rapidly, and later be livened up by pushing openings and curves with a knitting needle. These openings can be left to provide textural contrast or can be filled in with a contrasting yarn and/or technique, a process called *inlay*. Your long darning needle will work best here.

2. The inlay can be woven in various ways — top to bottom (easy to figure out) or from the outside into the center. To match up the completed weaving, start with the opposite weave and inlay an even number of rows. This figure demonstrates weaving a "lozenge" shape from the outside to the center.

3. Finished inlay: Inlay can be useful in integrating the various techniques, colors, and materials being used in a project. An application of inlay can be seen in Diagram 32 (4) (page 63).

D-13. *The double half hitch (macramé knot)*

1. The ridged lines of the double half hitch: This macramé knot, also called the *clove hitch*, produces a hard ridge that provides structural strength as well as textural contrast to off-loom work. Illustration 7 (page 47) presents a close view of the contrast between woven surfaces and ribbed surfaces of double half hitches. Here, two slanting, spaced-out rows of double half hitches start.

Working strings play two distinct roles in this knot. One string acts as a *holding cord,* while the remaining are *knotters.*

2. Filling a row to the left, slanting downward: The string selected to be the holding cord (X) is laid across the top of the remaining strings — all knotters — in the direction the ridge is planned to take, then must be held firm in that direction. If working free-hanging strings, hold the cord tight in your left hand when building to the left, as shown here, and in your right hand when building to the right. (You should learn to make the knot with both hands.) It is easiest to first practice this on the working board shown on page 36, where holders are kept taut by being inserted into slits cut into the edge of the board as they are needed.

The string next to the holder becomes the first knotter (Y). When it has made two loops over the holder it is dropped and the next knotter to the left picked up. Notice all the knotters begin from underneath the holder and emerge from the finished knot at a right angle to the knotted row.

A diagonal row of double half hitches can be performed anywhere, following some of the previous weaving, say, to make working strings pop into some angle and cause more shaping and colliding.

3. Knotting to the left and to the right: The start of each loop, where it passes over the holder, is made in the same direction as the row is building. So when building to the left as you are at 2, knotter Y starts forward to the left as it loops over

the holding cord, then circles back to the right as it goes under it and over itself. Repeat for the second hitch, which makes the knot firm. When filling to the right, then obviously you begin the loop to the right. Notice that the hitch follows the alternating over-and-under sequence of weaving — going first *under* the holder; second, *over* the holder; third, *under* the holder; fourth, *over* itself.

4. Finger positions: For speed, form the loop with the upper inches of the knotting strings and yank the tails through quickly. Starting to knot to the left is again shown here. Notice how the left hand stretches a taut length of holder over which the hitches are formed. If the holder goes slack when you tighten your hitches, it twists into the loops instead of riding straight through them, and distorts the knots. With your thumb in the loop, right-hand finger 1 passes the knotter Y back under the holder X to finger 2, which pulls down on the loop to yank the knotter's tail through. Then, pulling the holding cord out straight in the direction of the line wanted, slip the first hitch into place. Remember, hands trade positions when knotting to the right.

5. Establish the knot's position: Establish the knot's position on the holder with each first hitch and check that the distance the knotter jumps down from the last row is appropriate. The second hitch locks the knot, so hold the first in place while forming the second. Sometimes you want no space between rows when creating ribbed areas. With spaced-out, and especially slanting, rows, the distance the knotter jumps must be graded by eye with each knot. Usually the knots within a row are packed tight together on the holding cord, completely hiding it. So each successive knot is slipped up next to the last when its locking hitch is made. A final tug when the finished knot is in place (still keeping the holder rigid) makes it tight and adds a desirable crispness.

Concentrate on controlling the spaces between rows, achieving consistency in the knots, and economizing on finger movements.

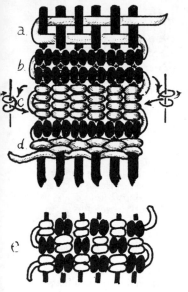

D-14. *Horizontal and vertical double half hitches contrast with weaving*

Here, a white horizontal working string intertwines with dark vertical working strings to create five different kinds of mixed and solid areas.

a. *Plain weave:* the black and white threads mix to make an even blend of tones. This woven area is flat and would appear speckled black and white close up, and gray from a distance. In other words, like stirring paint, your eye mixes the warp and weft colors when they are evenly broken in a section of plain weave.
b. *Horizontal half hitches:* the white thread disappears when it acts as a holding cord for a horizontal row of double half hitches made with the black knotters, and solid black horizontal ribs result.
c. *Vertical half hitches:* the white thread again travels horizontally across the dark, but this time as a knotter. Each vertical black string now acts as a holder to the white knotter. To begin, follow the diagram at the right and slip the white string under the far right black holder, looping downward to pass over in front, and upward to pass behind and make the hitches. Continue across, first slipping under, then placing a white double half hitch onto every black vertical as you come to it. At the end of the row, again follow the diagram to the side, and loop downward to start back over the first holder, then upward to pass behind it. Solid white vertical ribs result.
d. *Weft face weave:* rows of weaving are packed up tight to create a flat, solid white area.
e. *Checks:* black and white checks result when you alternate vertical and horizontal half hitches, and stagger the rows.

Appreciating the variety of surfaces that can result when threads intertwine allows you to achieve a great deal of richness using a very limited number of yarns and materials. Knowing how to make the changes makes it possible for you to orchestrate movements within movements as surfaces are linking one way, and forms another. The sequence drawings on page 63 also imply this possibility.

D-15. *A free line of double half hitches*

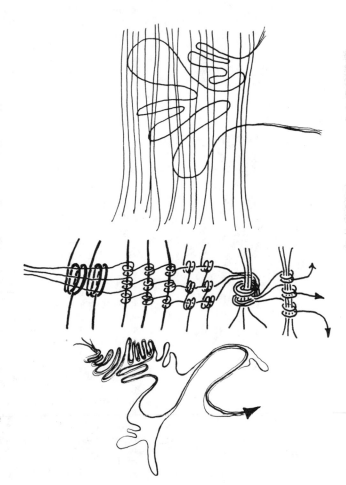

The following exercise can be implemented in a number of ways. The best way to discover the design potential of this versatile knot is to wander a holding cord freely over a group of knotters (at least twenty-four, all one color). The holding cord is actually made up of three individual strings, each a different color. Make very different curves with the knotted lines, and watch the rhythmic curves the knotters create as they go into and come out of the curved knotted line.

Build your line with both vertical and horizontal double half hitches as just described, playing the knotters and three holders through each other in every combination you can think of. For instance, in the center drawing, the knotters begin with horizontal double half hitches over all three holders acting as one, then the three holders separate to each make vertical double half hitches onto individual knotters. Still separated, and one-to-one, the holders make three rows of horizontal half hitches. Next, the three holders again group to become one cord and make a thick vertical double half hitch. Finally, the holders again separate, and build multicolored thick vertical ridges by doing individual vertical double half hitches over three knotters grouped as one.

Let the three holders go off on their own journeys temporarily, then reunite again, as suggested by the lower drawing. Later, you may weave into some of the trapped areas with open weave, to mix the warp and weft colors, and with tightly packed weave to create solid-color areas.

Throughout, think of yourself as creating lines and areas of different qualities: the lines can be thick or thin, tight or gradual curves, solid or broken colors. The areas can be ribbed or flat, solid or broken colors, large or small.

This exercise can be implemented in a number of ways. It could be considered an excellent warm-up to be done on a working board. Or, if worked into a large number of working strings hung from a rod, it could be a way of starting a large, free, exploratory piece. The possibility of very open areas combining with solid filled-in ones suggests it could be an unusual way to begin see-through projects like room dividers, window hangings, and large environments. The *indirect cylinder*, described on pages 67 to 69, is actually a three-dimensional variation of this exercise. The sculptural examples based on it may suggest more possibilities.

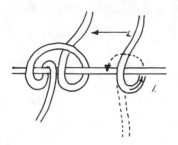
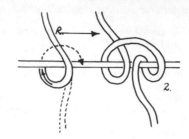
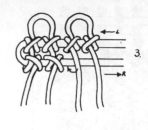

D-16. *Reverse double half hitch (macramé knot)*

When teaching the double half hitch to a class, inevitably someone gets a peculiar-looking knot by starting with the holding cord underneath instead of on top of the knotters. This is a wonderful time to launch into the "there's-no-such-thing-as-a-mistake" act, and to show that what was made is really a *reverse double half hitch,* a most valid knot, and particularly attractive when made into an area of closely packed rows. If you've already done some rows of double half hitches, look at the back of your work to see the crisscrossed texture of the reverse half hitches. Starting with the knotters on top of the holder puts the ribs to the back of your work. Knowing this, you can bring ribbed or crisscrossed areas to the front at will. Think of how useful this can be in building two-sided hangings, or any sculpted piece that has multiple viewpoints. The large lower fans in *Om* (page 74) have the half hitch ribs alternating between front and back surfaces.
1. Knotting to the left: When building to the left, first lift all the knotters up to hang in front of the holder — then loop the first knotter back to the right under the holder, forward to the left over itself and the holder, then again back to the right under and up over the holder. Pull down to tighten.
2. Knotting to the right: With the knotter starting on top, loop back to the left under the holder, forward to the right over itself and the holder, back to the left under, then up and over the holder. Pull down to tighten.
3. The crisscross texture of reverse double half hitches: You will notice that the horizontal ribs are behind the work, slightly raising this surface above the level of woven and ribbed half hitch areas.
Learning to be as fluid in making this knot back to front as you are in making it the usual way can be very helpful when sections of large pieces have to be worked upside down and inside out, as is the case with the upper parts of large cylindrical sculptures, described on pages 71 to 80.

D-17. *Finger weaving, starting at the right*

Finger weaving is also referred to as multistrand *plaiting* or *braiding,* since the threads continually cross back and forth through themselves to form the weave, just as in the familiar three-strand braiding. No separate weft is used. The perpetual-motion weave that continually feeds back into itself can start at one edge or in the center (Diagram 18) and can be loosely or tightly woven with contrasting strands to create different design effects that could be the topic of a whole book in itself.
Here the darkened string (1) that starts from the right-hand end of a group of even-numbered working strings traces out the route that all the threads follow when a strip is to continue straight, as is shown here. Eventually, this string will work its way back to the right edge, when it again folds left to continue the cycle. If the warps that slope down to the right are squeezed together, then the wefts never show. Diagonal stripes (also sloping down to the right) result when different shades are used.
To simplify the weaving process, use your left thumb to make the shed that this far right string — the temporary weft — passes through on a downward slope to the left. Your thumb always starts exactly the same, first over then under, finishing over. It stays in position while the weft is passed across just above it, as suggested at 2. When the first string has gone across, hold it on that downward angle while you pull all the strings it has just woven through into the opposite angle, sloping down to the right. The tail of thread 1 then folds back to join them as suggested by the dotted lines and shown at 3. Each row now repeats the process just described. It is optional whether to weave the threads trapped above this first row through themselves before proceeding, as they are shown doing here. The strings being worked here could be mounted onto a belt ring or buckle with graded shades of one color ranging from one side to the other, which will result in diagonal stripes when the belt weave is packed tight, as mentioned earlier. Or, the section pictured could be one of many starting from a dowel, which are going to be made to connect and separate in various ways in an experiment on shaping. For if you imagine weaving thread (3) back for a second row, which either follows the direction of its last one (up to the right) or goes across horizontally, and then threads are made to follow it, weaving now left to right, adding in or not at the right — you will see how the diagonal shaping principles at the beginning of Chapter III can make this technique break from the straight strip. The width of the strip can also be expanded by introducing a series of doubled-over working strings at the right edge to be woven down and added in lower left. Introducing at the left and adding in up at the right can also be done.

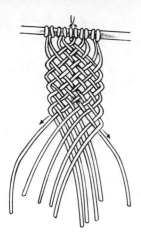

D-18. *Finger weaving, starting in the center*

Separate out an odd number of pairs of working strings, say five pairs (ten ends), as shown here, or seven pairs (fourteen ends). Starting with the center pair, fold the right-hand string over the left and weave it on a downward angle to the left. Then weave the left-hand string down to the right. Pull the strings you just wove through into the opposite angle to the weft that passed through them, so that they cross in the middle. Fold back the tails of both wefts to follow this opposite angle, then start the second row of weaving back in the center again, folding right over left, then finishing the weaves.

The methods of narrowing work and opening it up in the center pictured in Diagram 28 (2 and 4) (page 61) and the method of building a diamond, pictured in Diagram 30 (page 62) use this technique of weaving from the center out, so are very relevant when exploring this type of finger weaving.

D-19. *Twining*

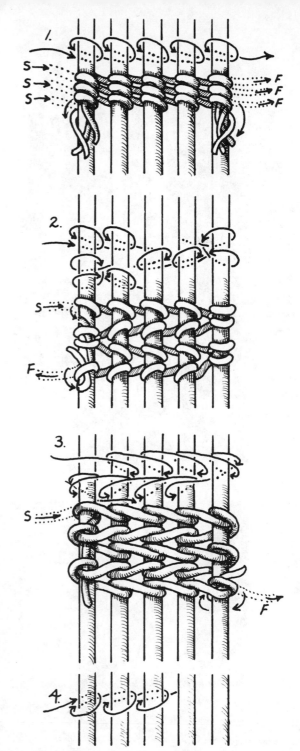

There are various types of twinings that are all characterized by the weft looping over the warps in some manner before continuing on. The same twining is often called by several names, so it's simplest to learn them by the nature of the looping.

1. Forward under two, back over one *(Egyptian tapestry knot):* This twining technique creates vertical ribs, similar in appearance to rows of vertical double half hitches, the only difference being that you make only one hitch onto each warp. If the work is going to be slightly open, and a consistent texture is wanted, then each row should be worked in the same direction. Shown here, a new weft begins each row at the left, and each loop is made above the weft. Ends are accumulated and eliminated along the edge warps.

2. As above, worked in two directions: When this twining comes to the end of a row, turn the corner with a double half hitch and come back in the opposite direction. Squeezed together, the rows look like 1, opened out they create a V shape, caused by the different slant of the loops.

3. Forward over two, back under one *(Soumak):* The texture of this twining is similar in appearance to knitting. To turn the corner, make an extra loop over the end warp. As in the above, the loops are made above the weft.

4. Create your own variations . . . by altering the twinings shown. Here, type 1 is altered by looping back below the weft rather than above it. If three or four loops are made this way onto each warp, a dramatic change of texture occurs.

Alan Russell

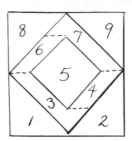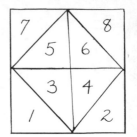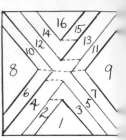

D-20. *The order for filling in the designs of the*
Bedouin Camel Decoration

I-3. *Twined* Bedouin Camel Decoration *(courtesy of Celia Chaikin)*

The twined strips of this *Bedouin Camel Decoration* were made with the Egyptian tapestry knot, pictured at 2 in Diagram 19 (page 43). Straight strips such as these can be easily worked, twining across a group of weighted threads as pictured near the start of this chapter in Diagram 11 (page 38). When twining or weaving geometric designs like the continually varied diamond motif seen here, it is easier to build up blocks of color than to weave across whole rows making all the color changes required. Your work is made easier still if the blocks of color build up in an order that doesn't interfere with subsequent color blocks. The drawings in Diagram 20 (above) indicate the sequence for building from the bottom up each section of some of the basic motifs from the Bedouin strips. Turn the drawing upside down if you want to twine from the top down, as may be the case if your twined pattern strip is to be part of a larger shaped piece developing down from a rod, which is being made with the weighted thread technique.

The diagonal designs used here avoid the slits that develop when design sections have vertical edges. Weft tails can be darned into the vertical ridges of the twining when you finish.

Buttons, coins, medals and metal chain have been sewn onto the finished surface. The strips were sewn together when they hung from the camel's side. This combination of decorative strips should be remembered when reference is made in Chapter IV to the possibility of grouping card-woven strips, whose quickly made patterned bands are similar in appearance to these twined ones.

Richard Harper

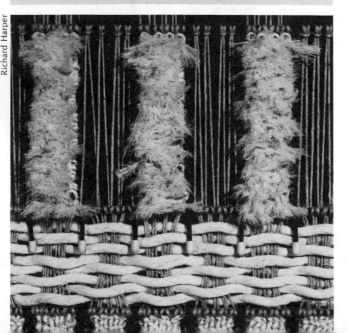

I-4. *Detail of* American Primitive, *by Shirley Fink*

This detail of a hanging, where jute and sisal rope join together rusted metal construction bars, shows the lower areas of twining providing pleasing contrast to the coarser textures of the weaving, pile *(Ghiordes knot)* and wrapping. A full view of this two-sided hanging appears on page 159.

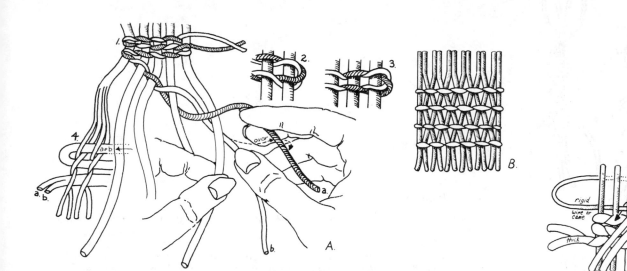

D-21. *Double twining (salish Indian twining)*

A. 1. In *double twining,* two contrasting threads twist round themselves in a figure-eight fashion, then pass over alternate warps, creating a dotted line that can build different kinds of areas. Here, color a was under the last warp, so now it twists over b to be on top of the next warp.

2. If the corner is turned by simply continuing to alternate the wefts, then the colors create diagonal stripes or a "twill" pattern. Imagine squeezing up the rows in 1 and you can see the diagonal stripes.

3. When the two wefts are twisted round each other once at the corner so that the same color starts the second row as ended the first, then vertical color stripes occur. A form of tapestry can result when two colors are thus carried and twisted the appropriate number of times to bring up the color you want, when you want it. This means that blocks of color can be built up, by one color twisting to stay behind for long stretches. Can you figure out how to make checks and horizontal stripes?

4. The warps can each be one thick cord, or two to four cords acting as one, as shown here. In this instance, you have the opportunity of making the passive warps trade roles with the two wefts, and themselves start twisting over the now passive wefts, which can be grouped as one or be taken across individually. This change to warp twining is the same principle involved in switching from horizontal to vertical double half hitches, so much of the variety suggested for it, particularly the taking-a-line-for-a-walk exercise, can be applied to this technique. Warp twining is the simple principle underlying card weaving, as is described at the beginning of Chapter IV.

B. Openwork: Select out an even number of working strings to work this variation on, and space them apart slightly. Start over one warp, then thereafter twine over two at a time, ending over one at the end. In the second row, and every even-numbered row, start over two warps and continue over two all the way. Row 3, and every odd-numbered row, repeats row 1. This staggers the location of the twining to produce a zigzagging grid.

C. Inlaying a hidden armature or third weft: A rigid material, such as wire or cane, can easily be carried behind your warps and get trapped inside each twist of the wefts. This material remains hidden if the wefts are thick, and the result can be standing sculpture or fiber baskets. If the rather unique tapestry possibilities of this technique are being pursued, this inlaid line could actually be another color of yarn, providing a third color option for the developing tapestry. At least two more color options can exist if doubled warps are different colors, and if you switch to warp twining to bring them to the surface.

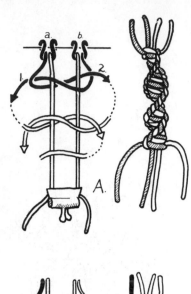

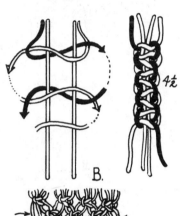

D-22. *Types of cords*

A. A twisting cord of half knots (macramé knot): Working with four strings, make the two center strings rigid by weighting them, placing them in a slit at the bottom of your working board, or just holding them with your fingers. Then fold the right-hand string (1) to the left across the two centers, holding it there with your right hand. With your left hand, fold the left string down over the tail of that right-hand string, then cross it underneath the two centers. At this point, replace your right hand with your left and, holding all the centers in your left hand, yank the tail of the left string up and over the starting curve of the right string. Repeat, always starting with the right-hand string. After four or five knots, the right-hand string starts twisting over in front of the work, toward the left side. Let it do this naturally, and bring the original left-hand string around behind your knotted cord to become the new right one. Continue as though nothing had happened, but start off with it doing the job the old right one did. This twisting action will continue, so you will be starting from the right with the other thread approximately every five to seven knots. The two centers aren't touched.

If two pairs of contrasting colors are worked with, a striped cord results, as pictured to the right.

B. A flat cord of square knots (macramé knot): A complete *square knot* is made in two steps. The first step is to make a half knot; the second step is to make the mirror image of the half knot. Begin the second part by laying the left rather than the right string over the centers, then finish with the reflection of the first step of the half knot.

Notice that the same string is always on top; here it is the light string that started at the right. Reversing the alternate knots flattens out the cord. Shown on the cord are four and a half square knots.

Below the cord of square knots are three rows of staggered square knots, made by dropping two strings at the edges of every second row. The knots made in the even-numbered rows are centered below every two knots of the preceding complete row, and draw on two threads from each of the knots they are centered under. The resulting area has an attractive open texture that can be altered by adjusting the distance between rows and/or the number of vertical knots per row (here it is one knot per row, but it could be two, three or four).

C. Wrapping: A wrapped cord involves simply winding one string around several, then threading the end of the wrapper with a needle, up through the finished cord. This becomes interesting if various colors run down the center, and a different color of wrapper is selected out of these center strings at intervals. Only the final wrapper has to be threaded up in a needle, the others just lie back into the developing coil.

D. A cord of half hitches (macramé knot): Another twisting cord results when one string makes a long series of double half hitches over several center cords. As in C, different colors can be brought out at intervals.

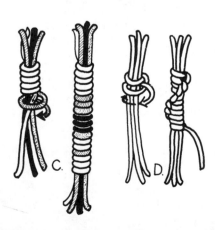

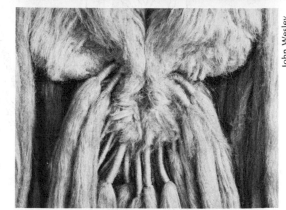

Anita Fisk

I-5. The Albatross *(7′ x 4′ x 2′), by Anita Fisk*

Twining combines with playfully wrapped and looped cords in this sculpture made of natural and dyed sisal.

John Wesley

I-6. *Detail of* Emanon, *by Karen M. Van Derpool*

A small section of wrapping gives a bite to this hanging, constructed from soft, unspun flax. The full view appears on page 168.

Mark Levensky

I-7. *Detail of* Untitled, *by Elayne Levensky*

Our eye is led out into space then back into the heart of the piece again, as ridges of double half hitches take off from the surface to become wrapped coils. The threads that form the coil return as one grouped holding cord to continue the flow of the line back onto the surface of the hanging with double half hitches.

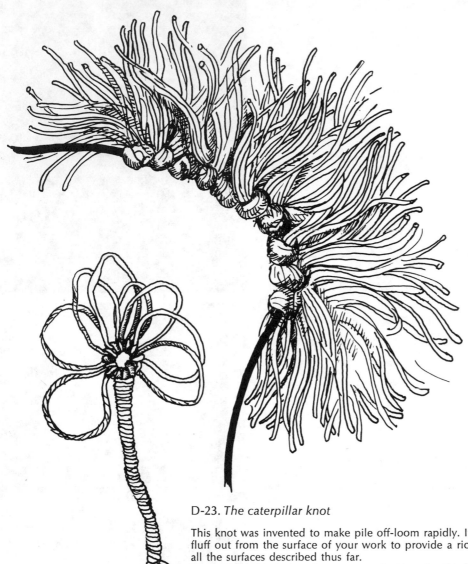

D-23. *The caterpillar knot*

This knot was invented to make pile off-loom rapidly. It can be used to make areas or lines that fluff out from the surface of your work to provide a rich, deep texture that contrasts markedly with all the surfaces described thus far.

You will be able to imagine many applications for this knot. A novel beginning for a piece would be to start from the standing caterpillarlike form this can produce. Or, the knot can be incorporated into a free-hanging project by using lines of it in a manner similar to the use of coiled and double half hitched lines pictured in Illustration 7 (page 47). The following text describes how a continuous line of the knot can exist on its own to leave the surface of the work or be continued along onto the surface by getting caught into, and being continued along with, a growing area of weaving or knotting or twining.

The pile results from cutting a series of loops which, if left uncut, can produce looped lines or areas instead. If the two ends of the line are bent round and wrapped together a daisy flower results.

A single thread of rug yarn made the caterpillar knot that produced the daisy pictured. The holding cord was four-ply jute. Wire could run along with the holder to produce a stiff stem. Clustering many cords as one, as is done to produce pile, would produce fuller flowers. Some raffia flowers interspersed with woolen flowers could be a pleasant play of shiny versus soft, as a whole bouquet of flowers pops from a spring hanging or out of a shaped coiled vase, made using the cylinder shaping principle; see Diagram 34 (page 64) and Illustration 11 (page 66).

D-24. Making the caterpillar knot

Cluster approximately ten ends of yarn to make a thick, plied, knotting cord about three feet long. Varied textures and shades of one color can be attractive — or ten strands of the yarn selected to be dominant in your project could be used.

1. This multistranded cord is shown making the already familiar reverse lark's head (Diagram 7, page 36) because when the ends are cut short, this also results in pile. Although this method makes good standing pile, it is slow to do. 1a shows a traditional pile knot, the Ghiordes knot, which can be seen in Illustration 4 (page 47).

2. Starting the caterpillar knot: Pile builds up fast, since this knot runs continuously, mounting one knot after the other onto a holding cord. If you are right-handed, it is easier to work the row of knots right to left, so knot the right-hand end of your pile cord to a holding cord (as shown here), so that when tightened, the short tail to the right matches the planned length of your pile.

3. The two loops that make up each knot: Your pile knotter starts to the left as if to make a half hitch but first makes an extra loop below the holder, then half hitches over the holder and down through that loop.

4. Finger positions: Your left index finger keeps the holding cord rigid while that first loop is made down under the thumb then up left to right over and around your second index finger. It is now easy to make the half hitch over the holder and down under the loop sitting on top of your second index finger. Yank the tail through and adjust the knot to trap a loop long enough to produce the length of pile wanted. Repeat this knot, building to the left till the row is as long as you want. Finally, cut the loops and fluff up the pile. It has already been mentioned that leaving the loops uncut is an option.

5. To incorporate lines of pile into an area in the process of being built, carry your pile knotter along with a weft or holding cord, and place a caterpillar knot in between every double half hitch, or weave, or twine, made with the background mass of working strings.

Replacing Run-Out Working Strings and Introducing New Ones

Introducing New Threads

The "obvious" introduction of new threads is referred to repeatedly in the following shaping principles, since this is a basic shaping device that can be employed continually throughout any off-loom project. Diagram 29 (page 61) shows four methods of gradually introducing new threads as work proceeds. The last drawing in Diagram 32 (page 63) shows whole groups of threads being introduced here and there as the project builds.

As a general rule, the introduction of new threads can be highlighted and presented most decoratively if the threads are introduced in an active role (see page 23).

Replacing Run-Out Threads

Start with threads two to three times the expected finished length to avoid their running out prematurely. The inconspicuous replacement of threads that are running out prematurely, however, is most easily accomplished if those threads can be maneuvered into a passive role by the time they have to be replaced. The replacing method generally used is to lay in the end of the new thread along with the old and carry the two together as one until the new one feels secure. Then cut off the unwanted tails behind your work. This procedure is similar to adding on in knitting. Make a point of tidying away tails immediately so that their presence doesn't confuse your study of the work for future direction.

Specific Notes on Hiding the Replacement of Run-Out Working Strings

Wefts and Twiners. The replacement of an exhausted weft with the same color can be hidden easiest in the middle of a row, carrying new and old together a few inches as already mentioned. To change color, introduce the new weft at the start of the row, fold the tail of the old in behind the new for about an inch of the new row, then let it hang out behind and continue the new on. Later darn the starting end of the new weft end into the work with a needle. Replaced wefts are most easily kept hidden when the warps are spaced close together, making the weft more passive in appearance.

Warps. Off-loom this replacement follows the same procedure as for wefts, since there is no tension on the warps.

Knotters (double half hitch). Either carry two as one, as mentioned already, or lay the old and new tails along with the holding cord and mount the double half hitch with the new string, knotting over the two tails plus the holding cord. Carry the tails with the holder for the next two or three knots, till secure.

Holding Cords

This is the easiest location to replace ends. I often devise to go into a row of double half hitches, or an accumulated edge (see page 60), when I see a number of working strings getting short. Just lay the new holding cord in with the old for a short distance before it runs out.

Half Knot

The two ends making the knot get used up fast if a long cord is being made. Fold the two old ends in with the center ones and lay the top looped end of a new pair of working strings behind all the center strings. Then bend the new right-hand string across in front of the centers — and go right into the knot the usual way, as if these ends were attached. The first completed knot holds the new strings in place, and the addition need not interrupt the twist.

III

OFF-LOOM SHAPING PRINCIPLES

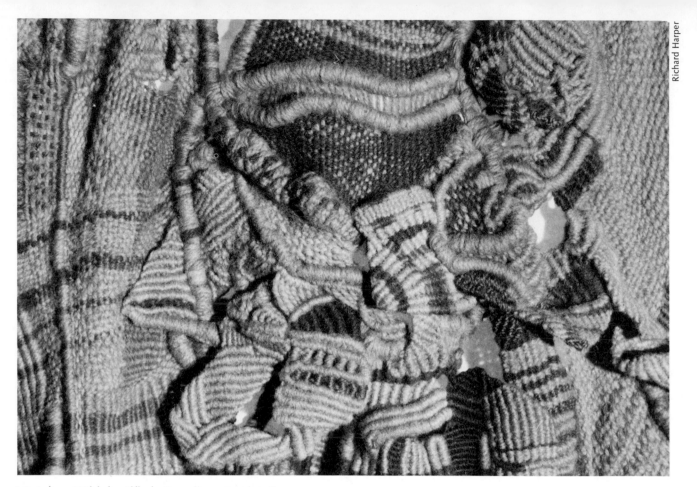

I-8. Jokers Wild, *by Elfleda Russell, center detail*

Walking to the right and left and using different shades of working strings to make double half hitches creates striped, ribbed flaps that stick out in front of the work pictured here. The hitches change from vertical to horizontal as changes are wanted in the color and the direction of the ridges.

Accumulated edges further emphasize the shaping by cutting out some of the resulting triangles (see particularly left center).

Going out of the picture, center right, is a long, narrow zigzagging strip that was first built about seven inches long by walking to the right and left, and then was twisted over before being caught back into the large mass of weaving that had, in the meantime, been progressing down behind it. Refer to the full view (title page) to see the relief effect of this.

Although this piece developed along the general lines of the working process, the following points made with respect to the process have equal relevance to any other method of working:

The thick ridges are the crocheted skeleton line being either mounted onto or double half hitched over or accumulated along.

Since it was felt ahead of time that a great deal of undulation and relief was wanted in the center of this piece, numerous new clusters of working strings were continually introduced into this section, either being mounted onto the skeleton or onto other existing threads. Purposely, more were added than there was room for, so that the areas they produced had to bulge out in front.

Large simple areas of weaving surround all this tangled activity to both contain it and provide the needed contrasts of large-scaled masses and quiet, smoother texture.

As you proceed with your own project, set yourself the task of changing the pace of your work by including both small, broken areas and large, simple ones.

In the upper center of this detail, long lengths of knotters trapped between rows of double half hitches were left to be woven into toward the end of the piece, when it was clear that some large dark contrast was necessary. This is an example of leaving doors open, described in the working process (page 22).

Learning to control a medium's natural tendencies to build shapes is one of the most important aspects of its study. The visual impact and/or function of a work is established to a great degree by its shapes, both internal and external.

When shaping is achieved as easily as it is where threads are manipulated off-loom, it is bound to be a strong characteristic of the medium and an important part of its study. An understanding of the basic methods of making threads change direction and start into forms is as vital to the student of off-loom as the techniques themselves.

Some of the shaping principles presented here can even be applied to threads strung into looms, and certainly off-loom shaping can be combined with on-loom weaving while work is in progress, as well as being used to manipulate a piece after it is released from the loom. So on-loom weavers can benefit from an understanding of these principles as well.

The shaping principles that follow are intended to guide you to an understanding of how you can consciously work up to shapes and, in so doing, can come to appreciate and develop the implications or the potential in the fall of yet unworked threads. Recognizing possibilities suggested by how the threads hang at the moment is, of course, very important in keeping the working process going, for each step is suggested by the last. The shaping principles can also help you understand how to develop and control an idea set before work starts or to control a form discovered in a partially completed piece.

As you learn how to make shapes expand and contract, move on the diagonal, and bend, bulge, cave in, fan, radiate, become

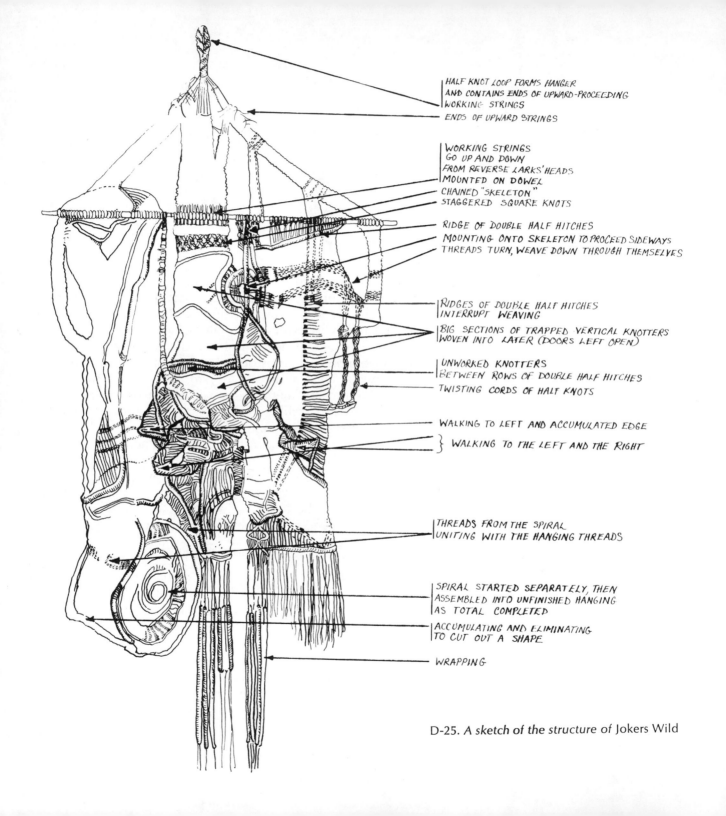

HALF KNOT LOOP FORMS HANGER
AND CONTAINS ENDS OF UPWARD-PROCEEDING
WORKING STRINGS

ENDS OF UPWARD STRINGS

WORKING STRINGS
GO UP AND DOWN
FROM REVERSE LARKS' HEADS
MOUNTED ON DOWEL

CHAINED "SKELETON"
STAGGERED SQUARE KNOTS

RIDGE OF DOUBLE HALF HITCHES

MOUNTING ONTO SKELETON TO PROCEED SIDEWAYS
THREADS TURN, WEAVE DOWN THROUGH THEMSELVES

RIDGES OF DOUBLE HALF HITCHES
INTERRUPT WEAVING

BIG SECTIONS OF TRAPPED VERTICAL KNOTTERS
WOVEN INTO LATER (DOORS LEFT OPEN)

UNWORKED KNOTTERS
BETWEEN ROWS OF DOUBLE HALF HITCHES

TWISTING CORDS OF HALF KNOTS

WALKING TO LEFT AND ACCUMULATED EDGE

} WALKING TO THE LEFT AND THE RIGHT

THREADS FROM THE SPIRAL
UNITING WITH THE HANGING THREADS

SPIRAL STARTED SEPARATELY, THEN
ASSEMBLED INTO UNFINISHED HANGING
AS TOTAL COMPLETED

ACCUMULATING AND ELIMINATING
TO CUT OUT A SHAPE

WRAPPING

D-25. A sketch of the structure of Jokers Wild

three-dimensional, you learn how threads can be trapped into permanent shapes by the very way they intertwine so that forms are dependent on, and a result of, the weaving process.

It is worth repeating the suggestion accompanying the fifth point of the off-loom working process (page 20), that just two or three of these principles can provide you with more variety than you can possibly explore, when combined with three, two, even one, of the previous techniques, on your first run through the working process.

As you study the shaping principles, remember that besides the possibility of incorporating the various shapings into work, each shaped element that results can be a possible way to begin a piece.

Employing repetition with variation, described on pages 21 to 22, can evolve still further variations of what follows. Each principle is portrayed here with a particular technique or combination of techniques. Realize that all of the preceding techniques can be applied to each case, and that a technique can change partway through a shaped element, suggesting many future possibilities to explore. Make a note of any variations that come to mind, for the potential is only touched on here. If you use some of the shaping principles with any variation of the working process, concentrate on the flow or transition from one principle to another. Sometimes this in-between section is actually another shaping principle being born.

Realize that the principles of shaping off-loom have been discovered as a natural by-product of working free-hanging threads with a playful and persistent desire to achieve forms. It would be more beneficial to acquire your own methods of building by letting the flexible yet purposeful spirit guide you rather than the details of each and every method of shaping. Perhaps using a few shaping principles in a first project will start to stimulate the recognition of other possibilities to the point where you feel capable of uncovering many more yourself.

The principles presented in this chapter may be integrated with the techniques of Chapter II in a variety of ways, only a few of which are described by the working process of Chapter I and the list of exercises that follows it.

Diagram 25 (facing) points to the techniques and shaping principles that make up the structure of *Jokers Wild,* seen on the title page. These are just some of the techniques and shaping principles described in Chapters II and III.

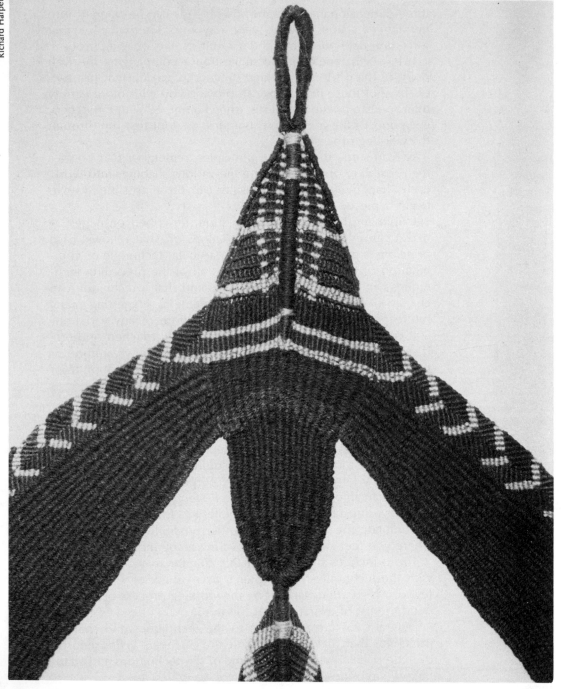

I-9. Stars over Bethlehem, *by Sally Graham, upper detail*

The attractive ending to the top of this piece makes repeated use of accumulating to the center to narrow work — as seen bottom center and as seen above — to deal with the coming together of the numerous threads growing up through the two sides. By eliminating as she accumulated through the center of the upper pyramid, the weaver retained just the number of strings needed to continue up into two strong cords of half knots, which meet at the top and trade tails as the final knots join the two cords to make a hanging loop. To read this weaving correctly, remember that the strings are being worked upward from the rod to finish at the top. The shaping of the central form that grows out of the lower accumulation is a good example of clustering warps to achieve changes of width and texture. Here, the weaver begins over and under many warps together acting as one, as can be seen by the width of the first six vertical ridges. Each of these ridges soon splits to form two warp clusters. Changing from six to twelve warp clusters not only slightly expands the work, it makes an attractive change of texture. Soon another split occurs, then eventually these central warps are spread wider as the side strings become involved, acting first as wefts, then as knotters, then accumulating as already described.

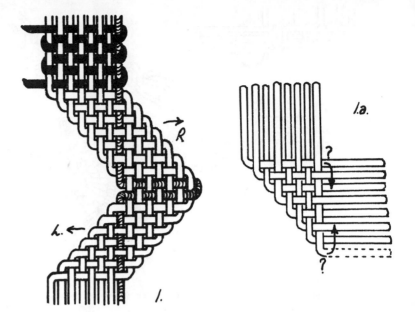

1a.

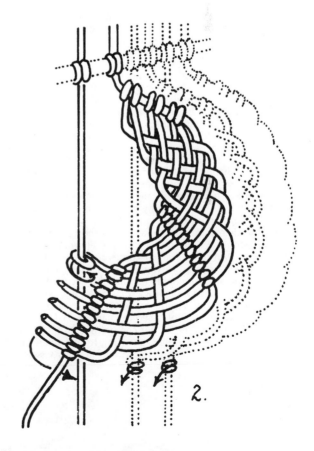

1.

D-26. *Walking a shape to the right and the left, moving on the diagonal*

1. The top section shows how weaving in the traditional sense, with a separate weft (black here) results in a vertical section of a constant width. However, this section will start "walking" diagonally to the right or left if one or the other of the edge working strings is picked up and bent to work across its group to hang down and be added in at the far side. The diagonal continues to the right as shown first here, as long as wefts originate at the left. The movement starts to reverse when any weft bends back to weave a second consecutive row, thus returning to the side from which it started. Here, walking to the left commences when the far right-hand string of the original group turns up at the left to be a left-to-right weft. Making a second row, it bends back and initiates the right-to-left weaving that walks the work back.

1a. A shape suddenly turns a corner to have the working strings emerge at right angles to how they started, by weaving across as described above but not adding in again at the far side. Each thread is left hanging after it has worked across. When all have finished, the decision can be made whether to bend the shape downward by starting to weave down the top string, or upward by starting to weave up the bottom string. The shape would grow out sideways if the top or bottom thread continued to weave up and down as a weft, or if a separate weft was introduced, or if these projecting ends continued weaving on to the right through other hanging working strings. Imagine how new working strings could be mounted onto the top projecting tail, then all weave down through the other tails to expand the width of this cluster. When introducing new threads at a time such as just described, where they immediately commence to weave, rather than tying a lark's head knot, it can be desirable simply to hook the looped end of each doubled working string onto the top projecting tail by bringing one end down in front and the other behind, so they start right into a weaving texture.

2. A winged shape can be made to fan out on edge in front of your work by mounting a few strings onto one vertical working string, then starting this shaping process but radiating each successive row to produce a turning fan. Occasional or repeated rows of horizontal double half hitches will give rigidity. Catch back onto another vertical string to trap the fan out front, when the shape has continued as long as you want. The suggestion of a series of such shapes, as shown here, would create an area of protruding ridges. See Illustration 17 (page 72) for use of this fan within a sculpture.

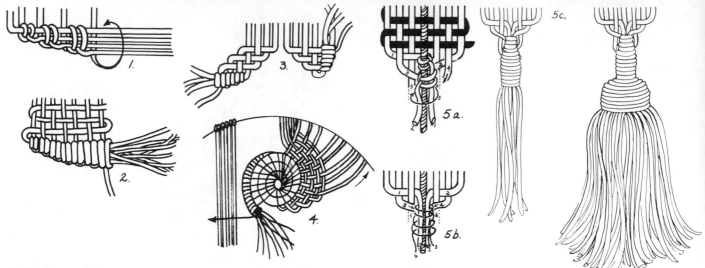

D-27. *Accumulating*

This method of gathering up ends is one of the most useful and dramatic ways of shaping. Three shaping effects can be achieved at once. First, the working strings abruptly change direction. Second, strings are suddenly squeezed together. Third, accumulating along an edge cuts out and strongly defines whatever shape you have just made.

1. Accumulating is actually done within a row of double half hitches. The only difference is that as each string completes its knot, its tail is folded up to follow the original holder, so that each successive knot hitches over the holder plus the tails of the preceding knotters. This causes the gradual widening of the row of double half hitches that makes up the accumulation along an edge, pictured here.

2. Ending an area of weaving with an accumulated edge cuts out the bottom shape of the weaving and squeezes the working strings together to pop out sideways, where they had been progressing vertically. Some possible ways to proceed on from here are: Do the "fanning" described on page 62 to make the maximum change from narrowing to expanding. Weave these ends down or up through each other, following the method of walking a shape to the right or left, described on page 59. The tail of the last knotter can bend up and become a weft to start weaving up and down through the projecting tails. The tails could slowly be spread wider, and your weaving gradually change from "warp face" to "weft face," as described in Diagram 28 (facing).

3. This drawing further elaborates on how the accumulated edge dramatizes shapes and causes sudden changes in the direction of your threads. You can find in the detail of *Jokers Wild* (Illustration 8, page 54) some examples of the accumulation on the right. Look center left for one particularly clear example.

4. Several messages are included in this drawing: A project can develop by starting with a spiral or cylinder (see pages 65 to 71), the tails of which continue on to start a larger thing going. Here we see half the tails weaving through themselves up to the right to attach to a shaped wire that replaces the dowel because of its ability to follow the lead of the curves of the spiral. Those ends can carry on any number of ways. Part of the spiral's curving edge is clearly sculpted by making an accumulated edge down the left side. The gathered tails can then weave through themselves out to the left, where they become involved with some other working strings. Accumulating and *eliminating* (Diagram 28, facing) can cut out part of a spiral, or make a hard edge around part of a finished weaving.

5.(a) Threads can be accumulated into the center of a shape rather than along its edges as we have been seeing so far. The working strings weave into the center, alternating from one side then the other, starting with the outer strings. The order of the strings is shown here: string 1 comes from the left, 2 from the right, etc., up to 6. Each in its turn makes a double half hitch over the center working string *plus* the tails of all the preceding knotters.

(b) Some threads can simply lay into the accumulation without making hitches first, to shorten the length of the accumulation. Illustration 11 (page 66) shows some tails of a cylinder gathered into three central accumulations. This method of accumulating can be useful for making temporary peekaboo openings in cylindrical sculptures or light fixtures. The openings can be closed in again with the fanning principle seen in Diagram 31 (page 62).

(c) Accumulating to the center can be used to finish off tails hanging at the bottom of a piece (or up within a piece). The finish can be complete when gathered tails hang from a series of side-by-side accumulations, or each accumulation can be a gradual way of gathering tails that are going to end in puffy tassels.

D-28. *Contracting or narrowing your work*

Here are various basic methods of narrowing the width of your work.

1. Altering warp spacing ("weft face" to "warp face"): The spacing out of your warps can be altered at will when you work off-loom. Taking advantage of this, by spreading them wide and squeezing them close, will not only alter the width of the work but can be used to alter the look of the weave as well. As shown at the top, when the warps are spread apart to expand your work, the rows of weft are easily packed tight to hide the warp, creating what is called a *weft face* weave. Conversely, squeezing the warps in tight to contract your work can completely hide the weft to create a *warp face* weave. In between, where the two appear in equal quantities, is a *balanced* warp and weft face weave.

2. Weaving to the sides and eliminating (center closed): This technique is actually a variation on the finger weaving seen in Diagram 18 (page 43), where warps cross at the center and weave to the sides. But here they are cut off at the sides to hang in a fringe. Eliminating them causes the work to narrow gradually. The left side suggests how the tails can be knotted into an accumulated edge instead of being cut off, to form a ridge that will follow and emphasize the narrowing edge of your work.

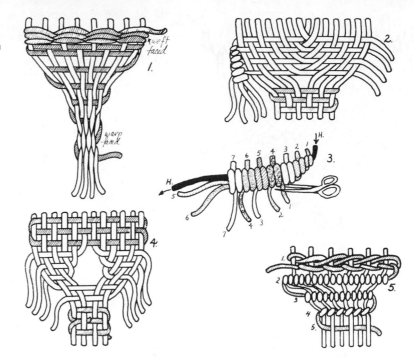

3. Accumulating and eliminating: Systematically cutting off tails after they have been accumulated through at least two following knots is a way of getting rid of unwanted ends. Notice that the original holding cord (H) remains throughout. Tails getting too short to continue can be worked into a conveniently placed accumulated edge. Parts of a completed piece can be outlined or cut out when this technique is used in finishing. In *Jokers Wild* (title page) the lower left was outlined this way. The detail of the spiral in Illustration 10 (page 65) shows it clearly.

4. Weaving to the sides and eliminating (opening the center up): Weaving the working strings from the center out to their own sides without crossing them as in 2 above results in opening up the center.

5. Narrowing by changing technique: Different techniques can be used for their tendency to affect the warp spacings in different ways. First, chaining the weft across the warps always tends to spread them apart. Second, triple half hitches, shown in the second row down, space the knotters wider than do the double half hitches in the third row. The type of twining that is really a single half hitch narrows it further. Finally, plain weaving can reduce in and in, as suggested back at 1.

D-29. *Expanding your work*

Besides using the natural reversal of some of the principles already described for contracting your work, expanding can be achieved by decoratively introducing new working strings (possibly of another color) into the midst of your weaving as it progresses.

Here are four different systems of adding into the same six original working strings. Each creates a different pattern at the point of being introduced. The order of colors in the final alignment also creates very different design effects as the weaving continues.

When the original and new warps are squeezed close together to produce a warp face weave throughout any of these adding-in processes, the resulting designs read out very strongly.

It should also be remembered that the occasional introduction of whole groups of threads all at once can also continue throughout the development of a piece to cause more sudden expanding than the gradual type pictured here. Various methods of introducing groups of threads are seen in the four sequence diagrams on page 63.

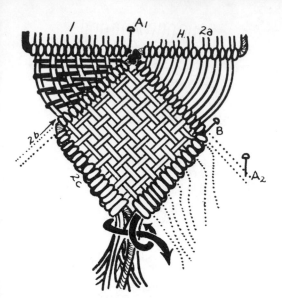

D-30. *Making a diamond*

Here is how a diamond shape can be made with a combination of weaving, double half hitche and accumulated edges.

Of the sixteen working strings to be used, the two original outside strings will act almost throughout as holders for double half hitches. Notice the left string is black here, the right is striped.

Begin by knotting seven strings onto the left-hand holder, to do section 1. Hold or pin that holder at point A_1 in the center to do this, and work the row from left to right.

Next, knot the right half of this top horizontal row (2a) by bringing the holder across from the right. Where these two holders cross in the center, double half hitch the left onto the right as indicated here by the black knot at the top of the diamond.

Then pin or hold this left or black holder at A_2 and knot all the knotting strings from section 2a onto it, working from the center out, or left to right. Do the same on the left (2b), filling the striped holder.

Starting top center, cross the first knotter from the right under the first from the left and weave out to either side. Continue this process until the diamond is woven.

Pin or pull against B and make an accumulated edge down the right side of the diamond. Do t same on the left (2c).

Let either of the original holders (shown here the black holder that began at the left) form this variation on the half hitch over all the other ends for a tidy finish. A half knot, Diagram 22 (page 46) would also work well here.

The fanning method that follows is one way of proceeding on from here.

D-31. *Fanning out of an accumulation*

A. Shown here is a means of fanning threads into wide, radiating curves where they pop out of an accumulation. Nonsymmetrical, as well as symmetrical, variations could easily be worked out by either working all the threads onto just one fan or by using different numbers of threads on each fan. Actually, any number of fans could appear at this point.

This is handy to practice first on the working board, where pinning can be done where shown here.

Divide your accumulated ends in half, and work first with only the right set. Of this set, select the most central string (or one whose color you want to hide) as a holder, and pin or hold it over the others so it slants up to the right. Knot the remainder of this set of strings onto it, making a horizontal row of double half hitches. Make an effort to tug hard on each first hitch so that no distance, or at least as little as you can manage, is allowed between the emergence from the accumulation and the knot.

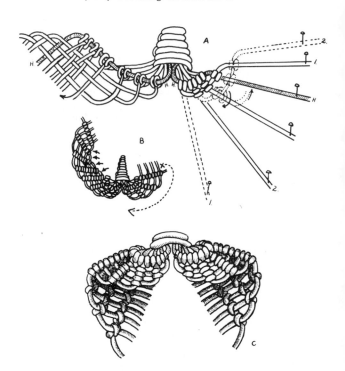

Next, pin all the knotters in a fanning fashion as shown. If working on the wall, strive to hold each holder in the position suggested here as you knot onto it.

Fold the tail of knotter 1 under string 2 and then double half hitch onto 2 with 1. Continue traveling string 1 across, being sure it acts as a knotter, and the tails of the previous knotters act as holders. In other words, make a row of vertical double half hitches, folding down the holder from the previous row to be the last holder in row 2.

Repeat the process, taking tail 2 across, so that now an increasing gap starts to appear between the vertical ridges. Making the fan requires controlling the distance between knots, so that with each row the distance becomes greater. You can see that the fan will continue growing upward as long as you want.

B. The left side shows the growth curve as the four knotters are in turn added in to produce four extra rows of vertical double half hitches.

On the right, the first holder is added in, but no knotters after that are added — bringing the process quickly to an end. Point X can then be folded down behind and attached to other working strings to form a three-dimensional wing that is trapped out front. Consider the possibility of folding down in front.

C. When both fans are folded behind and down as suggested above at X, this highly dimensional form results. The tails now face each other underneath on an angle that suggests the possibility of weaving a diamond, as shown in Diagram 30.

Students have worked out remarkably varied sculptures when directed to work with only the fan and diamond principles. You can see how one leads right back to the other.

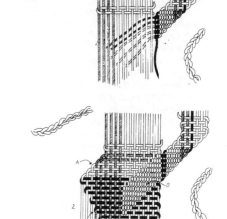

D-32. *An off-loom sequence: building step by step*

This sequence of four drawings shows how the off-loom process builds gradually, one step growing out of the last. It pictures ways of introducing new working strings and shows small sections joining into larger ones. The portion of the working process described on pages 22 to 23 refers to the methods of transition employed. The threads shown could be starting from the dowel or hanging out of previous work. Incorporating this sequence into your first experiment with the working process, or any other introductory project you have set yourself, may help clarify some principles of working sequentially.

1. A small section of weaving and double half hitches is walked to the left to collide with a larger section of vertical weaving.

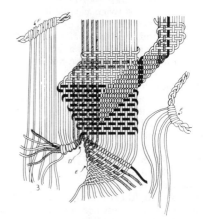

2. The weft of the large section is ended and replaced by the threads from the right-hand section that continue to fold left, weave across the center warps, then bend down to be added in and expand the far left edge (A).

Through this section of weaving, the slanting shape is apparently carried into the vertical shape it joins by the growth of a diagonal section of double half hitches made by replacing the weaving with knotting for some portion of the start of each horizontal row (B). The dark working string that comes from the right is chosen to signal some change every time it appears again. Here, when it becomes the horizontal weft, it bends back at the far left edge and continues weaving, bending back one warp sooner at the left end of each row, to slope the expanded edge back to where it started (C).

3. An accumulated edge starts curving left from a point that seems to continue the diagonal made above D. The black thread runs through a diagonal line of double half hitches that curves the knotters into an opposing diagonal, which is continued in the shaped weaving that follows it (E).

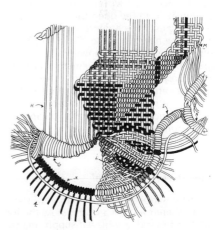

New working strings are mounted onto nearby sections of the chained skeleton line (F).

4. The accumulated edge continues left, gathering up the tails of new working strings (G); trapping unworked lengths of strings above H. Such an area of vertical strings can be knotted, woven, or twined into much later, as already described on page 22.

The working strings introduced at the right are wrapped together to start a coiled line (I) that flows across all the other working strings as a thick line of double half hitches, having all these new strings as a central holder (J). Clustering threads temporarily to make a multiple holding cord can provide a strong change of scale, even when all the threads used are a similar weight.

New dark threads are mounted with the expanded reverse lark's head to fill this line until it joins with the accumulated edge (K).

At two points, openings are poked into the weaving and dark lozenges inlaid (L), a tail continuing from one to squeeze a double half hitch onto the line already completed.

More new working strings are hooked on at M and then knotted over the skeleton line at N, as are tails coming from the center section. How would you proceed from here?

One possibility, shown, would be to fold one working string out of the accumulation at left, to curve back and around with a second line of double half hitches to follow and reinforce the long movement established already.

D-33. *One layer to two layers (double or tubular weave)*

Here is the principle of double weave, which is also used
extensively on-loom, or wherever more than one layer of weaving
is wanted to make anything from multilayered sculptures to
tubular or two-layered pillows, handbags, and clothing.
1. Alternate vertical working strings divide so that those the weft
passed over in the preceding row of plain weave are brought
forward to provide all the warps for one layer, and those the weft
just passed under are pushed back to provide all the warps for
a second layer. Here, the odd-numbered threads, shown light, make
the front layer, and the even-numbered threads, shaded, make the
back layer. Insert your left hand between the layers to keep
them separated.
Now the weft from the previous weaving proceeds back across to
intertwine with only the threads that make up the front layer.
It then circles behind to intertwine with the threads making up the
back layer.
2. Coming to the front again, the weft can continue circling, acting
as a weft, a knotter, or a holding cord, as it builds the tube.
Returning to a single layer will close the tube when and if that is
wanted. To do this, weave, knot, or twine the weft over alternately
a front, then a back warp.
This tubular weave can result in a very open cage or a solid stuffed
tube, or can be adapted to the spiral and cylinder forms that follow.
3. Transparent cage: As you see in 2, the vertical threads are
naturally spaced twice as wide in the tube as they were in a single
layer, if the original width of the work is maintained. If the weft
is a thick and rigid material, such as jute or sisal rope, taking it
round in spaced-out rows as a holding cord for double half hitches
will produce a round, open-textured cage. (Something of interest
could be suspended inside — a bird made of weaving and
macramé?) If the weft by itself won't hold the cage out full
and firm enough, wire can be carried along with the holding
cord, and if it shows, later wrap it with yarn or turn it into a fluffy
cage by attaching pile with the caterpillar knot, Diagram 23 (page 48).
The cage can now be expanded or made narrower by altering the
distance between the vertical knotters as they attach onto
the circling holding cord. The cage may become increasingly wide
and/or dense by gradually introducing new vertical knotters
in between existing ones.
This cage could exist in the midst of a large piece being built with
the off-loom process or could start a piece, such as a campy bird in
a gilded cage — all woven and knotted.
An alternative to the open cage is a solid tube. If the tube is to be
stuffed it must have a dense surface, which can be achieved by
introducing new warps (see Diagram 29, page 61) or by packing the
weft rows tight to make a weft face weave. The tube could slowly
expand by using both these methods of expanding.
Before closing the tube with plain weave, stuff the open tube with
matching yarn scraps, cotton batting, old nylons, even Kleenex,
toilet paper, newspaper, or lint from the dryer filter will do.
The spiral and cylinder shaping principles that follow are variations
on this principle of double weave.

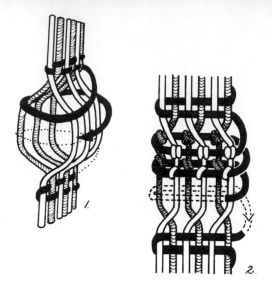

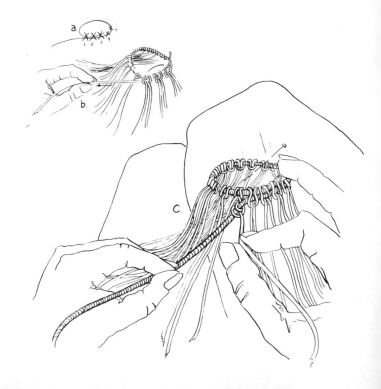

D-34. *Starting the spiral*

The text describes how this method of starting a spiral is only
slightly altered to start a cylinder. As the long holding cord circles
round and round, a firm, self-supporting shape results that has
many sculptural uses.

Spirals and Cylinders

The flat, round spiral and the tubular cylinder are based on the same principle of construction. However, there are many different ways to begin and proceed, and some examples of these follow. But first I shall describe a basic method of building them both, which shows their relationship and suggests how they can be combined.

Diagram 34 (facing) shows how both elements can begin from a loop made at the end of a long, preferably heavy, holding cord. This holding cord can be a finer cord doubled or tripled, wire, cane, or heavy one- or two-inch sisal, to name a few possibilities. The loop is filled with lighter-weight working strings, such as two-ply rug yarn, which are mounted onto the loop with reverse lark's heads to start a spiral and expanded reverse lark's heads to start a cylinder (Diagram 7, page 37).

Begin mounting as shown at *a*, where the tail of the holder first overlaps itself, making the first three lark's heads over both lines of the holder to secure the loop. When sufficient working strings are mounted to fill the loop of the desired size, then tighten the loop so no spaces are left between the lark's heads. Part *b* shows how to pull back on the holder while pinching the first three lark's heads in your other hand. The loop is conveniently pinned to your knee (put slacks on first!) as shown at *c*, and the tail of the holder begins to circle round and round, while the working strings knot, twine, or weave over it as it passes. In this diagram, knotting is the technique selected, and the last string mounted makes the first double half hitch of this first row. The mounted strings are shown spaced apart for clarity but would actually be packed close together, completely hiding the holding cord. The starting loop can be any size. If the spiral technique is being used to build a solid flat disk or plate, the starting loop may be tiny.

To build a cylinder, continue circling the holder, using only the working strings mounted at the outset. The constant number of strings makes the work build vertically.

To build a spiral, each consecutive row must be increased in diameter if the work is to lie flat. This requires the continual addition of new working strings, mounted onto the holding cord at intervals between the existing working strings. Frequency of added interval must be worked out with each

Richard Harper

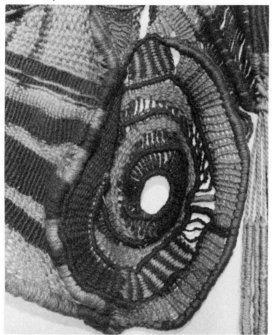

I-10. Jokers Wild, *by Elfleda Russell,* *spiral detail*

This spiral began on its own and was finished after being assembled into the large hanging, seen in full view on the title page.

combination of materials to see what is necessary to keep the work flat.

The spiral in Illustration 10 (page 65) was started as just described, but new strings were purposely added less frequently than would be necessary to keep it flat. The result is an abbreviated cone. Double half hitches were knotted onto the holder as it circled round in spaced-out rows. The working strings stretched between the rows were treated in various ways — woven into as warps, wrapped, and just left. The spiral was attached into the hanging as it was in progress by continuing to knot the working strings coming from the left of the spiral over the vertical working strings of the hanging — using vertical double half hitches that record the threads coming from the spiral to pull visually the spiral into the body of the hanging. The right-hand working strings were gathered up along the curve of the spiral with an accumulated edge to cut out that line.

Richard Harper

I-11. *A cylinder becomes a cone*

A fun hat, a basket, a vase for a bouquet of fiber flowers, a volcanolike projection for the face of a wall hanging, a hanging light fixture — these are some possibilities for this cone, which is actually a combination of the cylinder and spiral principles. If a long cylindrical sculpture or light fixture is planned, temporary openings can be made into the sides of the cylinder by accumulating into the center (page 60), as is done here on three groups of threads. Fanning out of the accumulation (page 62) could fill these openings in again later.

The shaped cone in Illustration 11 (above) shows the spiral and cylinder process combined. The tightly packed rows make

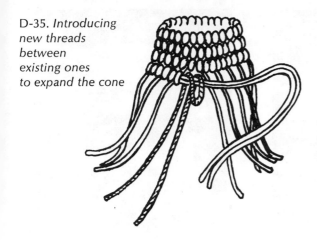

D-35. *Introducing new threads between existing ones to expand the cone*

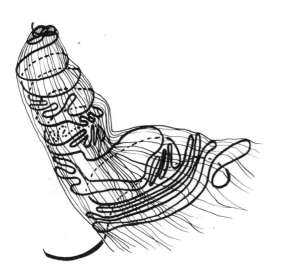

D-36. *Building an indirect cylinder*

This element can be the start of a three-dimensional variation of the off-loom working process, as seen in Illustrations 17 and 18 (pages 72 and 73).

a rigid standing body, and if the working strings perform double twining (Diagram 21, page 45) over a holding cord of cane, the result is actually basketry. Imagine the sculptural possibilities of this! The holding cord here is the heaviest jute available at the local hardware store (five-ply), doubled. The working strings are various shades of rug yarn doing double half hitches. To expand the walls, strings were added at spaced-out intervals after every fifth starting string (using the reverse lark's head) in the manner shown in Diagram 35 (left) and the central portion of Diagram 38 (page 70). Every addition was marked by a color change. After adding on in two different rows (remembering that double half hitches cause a row of expansion between every row of addition, as can be noted in Diagram 38, the walls continued vertically while the strings were rearranged to create patterning in the manner described in Diagram 39 (page 70). The work was expanded again toward the bottom, then the tails gathered into groups by being accumulated into the center (Diagram 27(5), page 60). Diagram 37 (page 68) shows how the diameter of this type of form can be reduced by temporarily dropping strings down the center or on the outside until they are needed again.

Stars over Bethlehem began as a class assignment, where students were to build a hanging combining spirals and the principles of expanding and contracting. A description by student Sally Graham of how this wall hanging grew out of two similar cylinders can be found on pages 80 to 81.

Reminiscent of African and Eastern ceremonial headpieces, Frances Allen Rosenblatt's *Siamese Hat* (page 68) is constructed entirely of spirals and cylinders, all made with the double half hitch. The main body of the headpiece is made up of one expanding and contracting cylinder, with smaller elements completed separately and added later. A round pebble has a cylindrical nest, and shells hang from the sides.

Francie came to fibers with a great deal of experience in various other media, and the headpiece is clearly a continuation of some very personal ideas of form and content that included, just prior to this piece, metal-worked breastplates and helmets. This novel use of off-loom shaping suggests applications of these techniques to costuming and props in modern theater and dance.

The indirect cylinder (left) is a meandering, organic variation on the basic cylinder. This undulating form can grow

I-12. Siamese Hat, *by Frances Allen Rosenblatt*

Francie models her hat, which was built entirely of spirals and cylinders.

I-13. Siamese Hat, *by Frances Allen Rosenblatt, back view*

Note the decorative fringe made by the cut ends of completed and assembled spirals.
The neck flap provides a change of direction to the horizontal ribs of the spiral.

I-14. Siamese Hat, *by Frances Allen Rosenblatt, side view*

The shells and pebbles provide a contrast of surface, and the shells make music as the head moves.

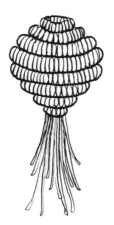

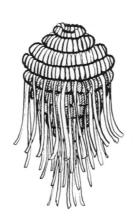

D-37. *Dropping threads to decrease the cylinder's diameter*

The decorative possibilities are self-evident, depending on whether strings are dropped inside or outside of the growing cylinder. If dropped strings are brought back in, as shown at the right, the cylinder can be made to expand out again. The solid form would then build inside a network of lines.

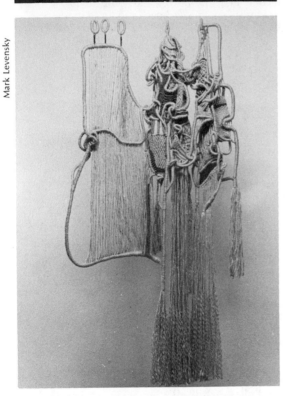

I-16. Untitled (3' x 7'), by Elayne Levensky

This sculptural hanging grew out from an indirect cylinder. Jute rope is combined with maroon rug yarn and heavy gold cotton cord. The control and imagination used to balance different types of areas are discussed on pages 69 to 71.

I-15. Cocoons (2½' x 6'), by Elfleda Russell

Built mainly of indirect cylinders (see Diagram 36, page 67), pieces were started separately, then assembled and completed. The full cylinder at left started at the bottom "head" area from a cluster of three or four loops locked into a starting knot. It was almost completed by the method shown in the following diagram (page 70), and then hung upside down from the ring. The open cylinder, back center, started the same way but was hung right side up from the ring and made to join in with the first closed cylinder. As it was completed it continued on to suggest a third fragment that was in turn taken up to a third point on the ring.

The tiny cocoon, right upper center, could have come out of the cup below and to the right that responds to its shape. It is hard, knotted and woven over a blob of rope.

The suggestions of full and tattered forms, and consequently stages of growth and decay, resulted indirectly from a concentration on the open and closed forms easily built with the indirect cylinder. The feel of organic forms and stages was emphasized after it was observed occurring naturally with the process of working.

from one or a number of starting loops. The holder continually interrupts its progress around the cylinder to take rhythmic side trips. New strings can be added, and worked through themselves using other shaping principles, as the cylinder builds. The curves can be varied as discussed with "taking a line for a walk" (page 15).

An interesting three-dimensional variation on the off-loom working process would be to start an indirect cyclinder, incorporating other shaping principles into the undulating form. It could then be assembled, along with other similarly started shapes, into a large sculptural composition.

Cocoons, pictured in Illustration 15 (left), was built in this manner. An effort was made to build open and closed organic cylindrical forms which, as they grew, began to resemble stages of metamorphosis, hence the title. A five-ply jute rope holding cord was combined with medium-weight natural flax working strings. The piece hung in a tree for a year, intimidating all the regular caterpillars. West Coast rain finally caused the full cocoon on the left to sag inward, but a paper bag stuffed inside has helped it recover its original form, and it has moved indoors. The discussion accompanying the photo details how it was worked.

Illustration 16 (left) was this student's first weaving adventure. Elayne Levensky was already an experienced designer, and needed only a few techniques and principles of shaping whispered in her ear and she was flying. This large hanging began from an indirect cylinder in the center and exploded in all directions. It is a wonderful example of varied

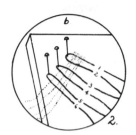

D-38. *Introducing into the center*

A decorative expanding shape of double half hitches results when contrasting threads are continually introduced into the midst of existing ones. This is the expansion method used in the cone pictured in Illustration 11 (page 66). Diagram 35 (page 67) shows how to start this expansion on the cone.

1. This type of expansion can occur anywhere within a larger piece, as suggested by *a*, or can be a novel way of starting either a whole work or a section to be assembled onto a larger piece, as suggested by *b* here, and shown in detail in 2 below. New threads are mounted with the reverse lark's head, and expansion capitalizes on the fact that the double half hitches that follow produce twice the number of loops supplied by the mounting. Consequently, it is only necessary to introduce new threads into every second row, as is seen occurring here in rows 2, 4, and 6, with natural expansion continuing in rows 3, 4, and also 2 (double expansion occurs here — the light thread could have been introduced in row 3).

2. This decorative triangle can be started on a working board, then applied later to a hanging-in-progress.

D-39. *Rearranging knotters to create patterning*

The patterning of the sides of the cone pictured in Illustration 11 (page 66) makes use of this rearrangement of knotters as a way to depart from continuous stripes made by the multicolored knotters and to produce, instead, patterning.

Here, the knotters maintain the starting order through the first three rows, but start being rearranged to build row 4. As the holding cord moves from right to left in this row, a light knotter is applied, then the right-hand one of the two central dark knotters is crossed to the right in front of the light knotter set up to be used next, which places a dark, rather than light, knotter second on the holding cord. The light thread skipped over is knotted next. Then you can see that the light knotter to the left of the remaining central dark knotter must be crossed to the right behind the dark thread, and knotted next. Finish the row with first the dark knotter, then the remaining light knotter. Continue rearranging, always making the pattern threads (here dark) pass in front of the background threads (here light).

This rearrangement can be used to produce elaborations and focal points in a developing project.

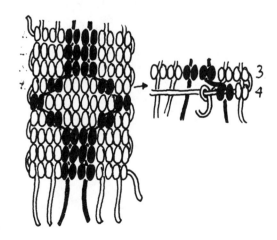

masses offsetting each other. Notice how the large simple shapes on the left balance the highly convoluted, dynamic area on the right. Also, notice the two contrasting qualities of line and form repeated throughout — tightly curved and straight-squared. This weaver has combined imaginative shaping with a sensitivity to change of pace and proportion. The swelling of the simple area on the lower left balances the activity of the upper right in an unexpected manner. This use of surprise combines with a sensitive use of detail to catch and hold a viewer's interest for some time.

Building Symmetrically on Wire Rings and a Description of *Om*

Two total views of the sculpture glimpsed in Illustrations 17 and 18 are seen on page 74.

This piece was gradually worked out by looking for each new step in what was suggested by the last, so the overriding goal was the same as that already discussed in the off-loom working process; that is, to exploit the capability free-hanging threads have of changing direction, changing roles, and building self-supporting forms, and to seek a final form through the process of working itself.

The idea here was to shape with the weaving and knotting so that forms of fiber project far beyond the rings. The resulting sculpture would start from a full base but continue on to undulate with more variety than is possible when the form depends entirely on the rings for shape.

The following discussion of how this piece evolved includes the technical information needed to start a shaping project from rings rather than a dowel and outlines as well some of the factors that come into play when symmetry is used.

Starting in the Middle

It can be faster and easier to start a large cylindrical piece in the middle, rather than at the top or bottom, for that avoids the need for excessively long working strings. Twenty- to thirty-foot-long strings would have been necessary had this

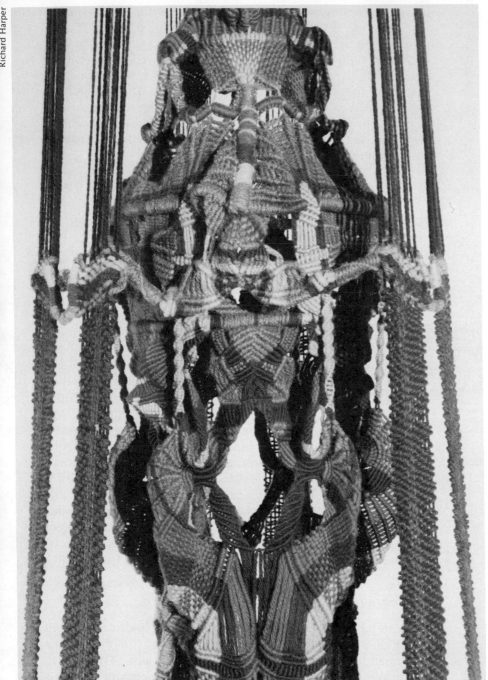

I-17. Om, *by Elfleda Russell, center detail*

Here is a detail from a symmetrical variation of the off-loom process, worked on wire rings. The long sculpture grew down and up from the center ring — see Illustration 18 (facing). Most of the shaping principles described already are at work on weaving, double half hitches, and half knots.

I-18. *Starting* Om

Forms start to build downward from the midpoint starting ring. After continuing down a little farther, new strings were mounted between existing ones and worked upward. Support strings attached to the ring are temporary; those holding the fans were covered with cords of half knots and incorporated into the sculpture as it grew upward.

piece started at the top! The ten-foot strings used instead were faster to work, and because the piece was worked suspended in the center of a room, the threads had sufficient room to hang to the floor without tangling.

Ends

As mentioned already, winding ends into butterflies is not recommended, because of their interference with your viewing of the fall of the threads out of previous work, which should be providing good clues on how to proceed. Ends not being used at the moment can be clamped out of the way with a few of the paper clamps pictured in Diagram 11 (page 38).

Choosing Colors

Since forms were going to be played up in this piece, it was decided to choose closely related colors that wouldn't distract

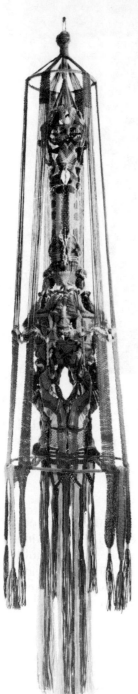

I-19. Om *(10' x 2'), by Elfleda Russell (collection of Dr. Richard and Mrs. Mary Anne Brodie)*

The "open view," repeated three times round the sculpture, exposes the original centers, also seen in Illustration 17 (page 72).

I-20. Om, *by Elfleda Russell*

Here you see the "closed" view that partially blocks the secondary centers, shown just started in Illustration 18 (page 73). This view alternates with the open view of Illustration 19 three times round the sculpture.

from the shaping. Colors with blue in common were selected with a broad tonal range. Deep purple (dark tone), electric blue (medium tone), lime green (light tone), and avocado green (medium tone) were decided on. The avocado was necessary to create a gentle transition between the bright lime green and the purple. If you mixed the red contained in the purple with lime green, it would tone it down, and the result would be avocado. The avocado is rug yarn, the remaining colors are Woolworth's knitting worsted. Two four-ounce skeins of each color of worsted and a half a pound of rug yarn were selected. (A lot was left over.)

Making the Rings

Medium-weight galvanized wire was obtained at the hardware store. It was tested for ease of shaping and the strength to maintain a form. The first ring, approximately a foot and a half in diameter, was made by circling the wire round three times for extra strength. The ends were held with adhesive tape. Electric blue wool worsted fabric was cut into long half-inch-wide strips, which were wrapped round the ring to cover the wire before starting. A needle and thread sewed the ends firm.

Hanging the Rings

Temporary support strings were attached at three equal-distant points on the ring (Diagram 40, left). They were in turn attached three feet up to a single central hanging cord, which was attached to a ceiling light fixture. The hanging cord was arranged so that the work could be easily raised or lowered as it progressed. A simple pulley would be worthwhile installing if much work of this sort is to be done. If a pulley is used, your hanging cord can be anchored to a doorknob, a table, or a chair. You will sometimes want to stand as you work, other times sit. Work should be easily adjustable to a comfortable working or viewing height.

Mounting Working Strings to Start Down
(Three Symmetrical Centers)

It was decided here (which, of course, isn't always necessary) that the threads would be mounted to make three repeats of a symmetrical arrangement. The three temporary support strings

D-40. *Mounting threads symmetrically on the mid-point starting ring*

Here the starting ring is shown suspended from its three temporary hanging cords, with the central hanger going over an optional pulley at the ceiling fixture. The mounting of colored working strings can grow out spontaneously from the three equidistant points (original centers) and build to meet at secondary centers. Plastic or an old sheet can be placed on the floor under your work to keep the long ends clean.

Note that this process could be used to build a long cylindrical light fixture. Light bulbs could be inside, or fiber optics could poke through openings.

already located the center points from which to begin building out the symmetrical arrangements. Some thought was given to the quantity and position of each color as the arrangement grew, mounting with the reverse lark's head.

The three symmetrical arrangements were added to until they met, creating what was thought of as three secondary centers. Since the threads now being mounted were to be worked down only, they were spaced slightly apart to allow matching threads to be mounted in between, later to be worked upward.

Some Hazards and Bonuses of Working Symmetrically

I've already described the similarities between the off-loom working process and what was done here. However, dealing with symmetry does inject some big differences into this method of working.

First of all, the mere use of symmetry quite naturally contributes such a degree of balance and stability that any hopes of conveying dynamic movement have to be worked for extra hard. I was constantly battling against the natural rigidity of symmetry by striving for surprise and unexpected forms that would lead strongly away from vertical and horizontal lines. The shaping method of fanning out of an accumulation (presented on page 62) was discovered here as a result of this effort to build diagonals and curves. It was exploited in variations throughout the piece.

Second, there is a bonus attached to working symmetrically. Every time you make the reflection, or mirror image, of one half with the other half, trapped between in the center — sometimes as negative spaces, sometimes where forms join — is some unexpected by-product of your work that can feed added information into your vocabulary of forms and always doubles the number of possibilities to consider in the next step. Because now you must decide whether to continue the flow of the positive or negative, the direct or indirect, forms that resulted from the last step.

Saying this, and having you view the finished product, may overwhelm you with how complicated it all looks. Remember that a piece like this grows bit by bit, decisions only have to be made one at a time, and that isn't so difficult to handle.

Studying Your Work and Establishing Dominant Qualities

Continually turn your work to study all the viewpoints that are developing, as you decide on the next step. A secondary form just around the side can sometimes be quietly growing into a more interesting shape than the one you are concentrating on. You may want to shift emphasis.

Toward the end of a piece, decisions start to get more difficult. Whatever you do then must accommodate a growing number of previous decisions. There always comes that turning point, where it is time to stop introducing more new elements and begin pulling something out of what has happened thus far. Attempts to tie parts together, emphasize qualities or a shape, usually involve making variations on what is now present in the piece. Don't hesitate to undo work.

Inventing and Repeating

Here, one center was worked for a short distance, then copied in the other two repeats. It was fun working things out the first time, but tedious repeating them. One of the problems of working symmetrically is that you have fun only part of the time.

Leaving Parts Unworked

I've already talked about the advantage of keeping openings in your work that can be worked later when you better see what is needed. Within the neck of the central figure of *Om* many sections of warp were left trapped between widely separated rows of double half hitches, and later woven or knotted into as seemed appropriate. (See Illustration 21, page 79.)

Note one further method of leaving the doors open that was used here. Two sections of work were built out so far, then the working strings left hanging while the piece proceeded on elsewhere. The plan was that these sections would build indepently in front of the piece and later get caught into some other parts of the work that didn't exist yet. Exactly how and where this connecting would be done wasn't known until the time seemed comfortable for doing it. Several times I checked the possibility of attaching the fans up before they hung well, and so were fixed. And the arms that catch into the outer curtain turned out to be a fortunate method of integrating the inner and outer activity. At the time of leaving those ends, it wasn't even known there would be an outer curtain, it was only felt that whatever major things were going to happen should happen in this general area. (Illustration 17, page 72, focuses on this area.)

Working Upward

After the lower portion developed a little below the large fans, the bottom was left to be finished later and threads were mounted on the ring between existing mounted working strings, to start building upward.

One has a choice of hanging the piece upside down to work from the center up, or, as I did here, to keep the work right side up but fold the upward cords out and down and work short sections at a time — inside out and hanging upside down. Fold these finished sections up and clamp them to the temporary hanging cords to view your work and plan the next move. The method of working double half hitches back to front, seen in Diagram 16 (page 42), can be helpful here.

It means you are flying blind to some degree while doing these upward parts, but sometimes interesting things happen that way and, in the long run, it's easier to keep track of the whole shape that is evolving. Clamp the upward sections to the temporary hangers, raise the piece, then stand back and squint to subdue detail and study the overall form.

After about five inches of working upward, the fans had already been caught up into the sculpture, and a second larger ring was attached. Shortly thereafter, a very small ring was also added, to reduce into the neck. A slightly wider ring helped swell the head form out again near the top.

Adding the Outer Curtain

When the form hung nearly finished, it seemed desperately disappointing. All I could think of was that it was so obvious. I came to realize that what was wrong was that the whole form was too equally and too easily accessible. Nothing was being kept back to entice the viewer in.

I realized then that making parts of the piece fold over itself,

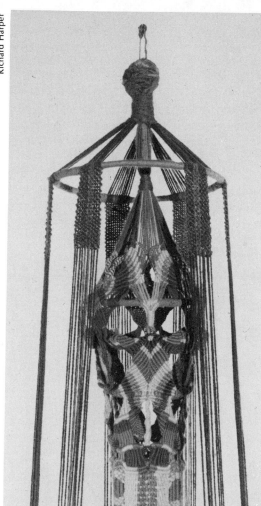

I-21. Om, *by Elfleda Russell, upper detail of open view*

or overlap, was an unconscious attempt to draw the viewer into the piece by not allowing everything to be seen from one distant viewpoint. As hindsight revealed that stimulating the viewer to explore was the purpose of hiding parts of the piece, it became obvious that not enough was hidden yet.

It now seemed necessary to set the jewel at a distance — by virtually putting it away in a box. Or, as was finally settled on, to tantalize by building around it what amounted to a fence with knotholes. So the decision to make an outer curtain was arrived at, to hide partially the most interesting form, to provide an initial impact of dominance and subordination that was now lacking, and to reward the viewer who responded to the invitation to come on in with the discovery of more and better things hidden inside. The title itself implies that the essence lies inward.

The top outer ring was suspended from the top cluster of upward threads that were gathered into a topknot only at the very end.

The threads used to make the curtain were finally found after a lot of trial and error. It was clear that the interior threads must not be used, but introducing anything new created a distraction. Finally, much deeper shades of the interior threads worked perfectly. Their treatment was kept simple to increase the effect that they serve as a barrier that the viewer is impatient to get around. Threads for this outer curtain were double half hitched onto the small upper ring and likewise knotted to the lower ring with great care taken to hang these rings level.

I've already mentioned that threads had been left hanging and unworked in the original center portion. As soon as the outer curtain idea struck, it was obvious that these could be worked into the curtain to provide transition and a clue to what lay within. Where these clusters of threads weave through the outer band of weaving, their tails are taken into accumulated edges that join and trade tails within the last knots at their center.

The decision on how long to continue the bottom center was made after this outer curtain was completed. Gathering the puff of top threads into a hard wrapped ball was the last step. See Illustration 21 (left) for a close view of the upper section.

79

The Final Results: "Open" and "Closed" Views

Full view 1 of *Om* (Illustration 19, page 74) shows the open view that exposes the original centers. The photograph that begins this study (Illustration 17, page 72) is a center detail of this view.

Full view 2 (Illustration 20, page 74) shows the closed or partially blocked view of the secondary centers.

The piece contains three of each of these views, and as it turns in the air, the view is alternately open, then closed.

Shaping Principles Applied to Clothing, Body Coverings, and Ornaments

Off-loom shaping principles can be easily adapted to clothing projects. The best way to work is directly on a mannequin — or a good and patient friend — summoning the appropriate shaping principles as they are needed. An alternative is to cut a paper pattern and choose a place to start, shaping as you go. A good method of joining front and back pieces at the sides is by using the "accumulation to the center" process shown in Diagram 27 (page 60), also eliminating as you accumulate (Diagram 28, page 61).

A Student's Experience with Shaping

The shaping study concludes with a description by Sally Graham of how her hanging, *Stars over Bethlehem,* was constructed by having a variation of the off-loom working process take off from two similar cylinders. This hanging was the result of an off-loom class homework assignment to explore and combine two shaping principles: making a three-dimensional cylinder grow larger and smaller, and making two-dimensional work expand and contract.

Our homework was to use one shaping technique to be the main idea of the piece, and to use the second shaping technique for contrast. My piece began with the two small cylinders at the centers of

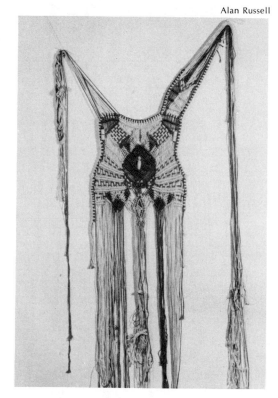

Alan Russell

I-22. *A vest in progress, by Mary Anne Brodie*

This vest for a teenage chess champion is being worked over a foam rubber pad so threads can be pinned to follow a paper pattern. With the back almost complete, the front right side is seen starting at the top. Strings can be added and subtracted as shaping dictates.

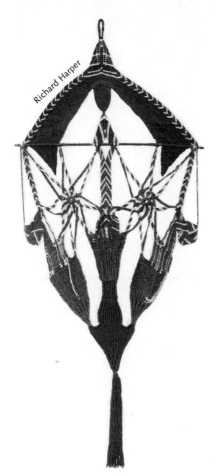

Richard Harper

I-23. Stars over Bethlehem
(4' x 8'), by Sally Graham

the stars, and extended into flat, narrow strips of double half hitches, which interwove to make the points of the stars. Then a triple arch, using the cylinder technique, was added to the piece in the center, and after that the two-dimensional principles of expanding and contracting and shaping to the side dominated the piece.

The stars were made and then hung on a rod, and the large flat areas were accomplished by weighted warp weaving. I did not plan my piece ahead of time, feeling that I was in a developmental stage and could learn a lot from the piece itself if I did not impose limitations on it beforehand. I would work "blind" and then stop and try to relate shapes and lines that had developed thus far, before proceeding again. When I looked at the stars hanging on the rod, all the lines in them were equally important. I drew what I had in front of me on paper, and tried finding lines of movement that flowed through the stars and the central arches that could be emphasized by being continued into the portion to go above the rod. My eye picked up two main sweeps. I continued drawing, trying different overall shapes for the whole piece. I wanted to break the finality of that horizontal rod, so I drew several designs for a top which would come up over the rod. I tried to pick up and continue in the shape of the top those lines I had emphasized in the stars. I continued the edges of the shapes and made them reflect the lower ones.

The center strip, to which the three small arches were attached, also ended abruptly at the rod so it, too, was continued in the top part.

The execution of the weaving in the top part of the piece depended on the center strip, and on the outer strip of double half hitch chevrons for its foundation. The open warps of the center strip were woven over by long wefts which double half hitched on the rod, came weaving through the warps of the center strip, and bent down to the rod again. These wefts then became warps and were woven over with a needle so that, at the chevron selvage, the weft could be attached. The leftover threads which have been half hitched around the rod were macraméed into a shape which filled the triangular space between two areas of the stars, thus greatly helping to erase the horizontal line of the rod.

The bottom half of the piece was worked in the same manner as the top half, finding inherent shapes in the work, drawing them, then finishing the drawing several different ways to select what seemed best.

IV

CARD WEAVING

An Expanded Off-Loom Technique

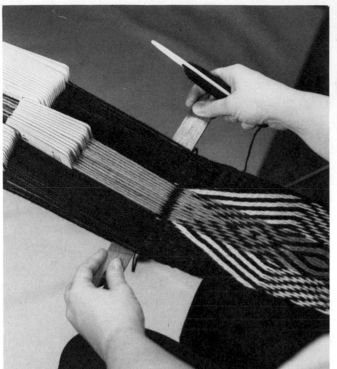

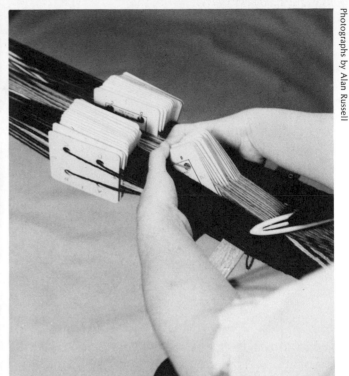

C ard weaving is developed extensively here to demonstrate how the potential of any of the off-loom techniques can be stretched by applying various shaping principles and implications transposed from other weaving methods. In fact, ideas virtually snowball when traditional card weaving is viewed in the context of the free-hanging techniques and their shaping principles, and of multiharness on-loom weaving as well. An expansion of a technique, and indeed of any of the elements you work with, follows almost of its own volition when you change your focus from broad to narrow and force yourself to work with a limited means, at least temporarily.

This expansion of card weaving includes:

— Some new developments on two traditional pattern methods.

— Card weaving acting like a four-harness loom.

— Three-dimensional and shaped card weaving.

— A method of combining multiple strips of card weaving with the free-hanging off-loom techniques.

The Nature of Card Weaving

A glance at Diagram 44 (page 94) shows a weaver sitting at a pack of strung cards, preparing to weave. Notice that each square card in the pack carries four warp threads, one through

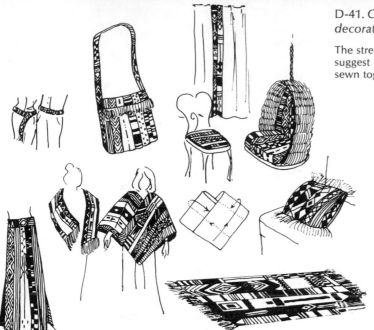

D-41. *Card weaving used for clothing and interior decorating*

The strength of this weave, and the decorative surfaces available, suggest many practical applications for strips used individually or sewn together.

I-25. Tribal Cloth *(6' x 10'), by Lillian Elliott*

Numerous strips of card weaving are sewn together to produce this evocative hanging of wool and mohair. Threaded-in patterns make some strips, natural fleece pops from the surface of others. Lillian Elliott was one of the first to explore card weaving as a flexible art form. Another example of her unique exploration of the technique can be seen on page 157.

Stone and Stecatti

each of four corner holes. The weft passes back and forth through the natural separation of warps, and weaving develops by turning the pack of cards forward and back.

The fabric produced is traditionally a thick, warp-faced, four-ply cloth, made as the four warps of each card twist round each other in rhythms established by your turning, and trapped by the weft. Card weaving is actually just an elaboration of the warp twining version of the double twining pictured in Diagram 21 (page 45). If you can think of those four warp threads twisting together round consecutive wefts, then you can picture in your mind how the four threads strung through a single card twist round each other to bring the desired combination to the top surface as you turn the cards to weave. A pack of strung cards just allows you to twine many sets of warps at once, completely automatically if you wish. And those cards aren't joined together, which means you have the option of turning them individually or in separate groups to bring different warp colors to the surface in different rhythms across the pack, allowing awesome flexibility in the orchestration of patterned surfaces. The unjoined nature of the cards also means the pack can split apart and break into weaving gymnastics that result in the three-dimensional and shaping possibilities described later.

Various shapes of cards can be used; however, I am concentrating entirely on square cards because of their ease of handling and versatility. One could extrapolate on the principles presented here to figure out how to weave the three-, five-, six-, and eight-sided cards also sometimes used.

Three Pattern Methods Compared

This discussion of card weaving begins with pattern. There are three fundamentally different systems of preparing and weaving cards to achieve patterns.

The first of the three methods of pattern weaving involves threading every card in the pack the same way, with two contrasting colors. Patterns are woven through various turns and arrangements of the cards. The manipulation of the cards, then, establishes the pattern in the *two-color manipulated weave*.

The second pattern system differs in that the pattern is threaded right into the cards, and turning can be more automatic. Here cards are threaded differently following a design chart you prepare ahead of time. The woven pattern, though altered by the turning, is established mainly by the threading, and is called here the *threaded-in pattern weave*.

In the third pattern system, some card holes are left empty, causing the weft to appear at points on the surface of the weave. The pattern depends on where the wefts show on the surface. The process variation featured here shows how this technique can exactly duplicate four-harness on-loom patterns, and is referred to as *four-harness patterns woven with cards*.

The Two-Color Manipulated Weave

We begin with the two-color manipulated weave, since the threading process is extremely rapid and you can get into the heart of the card weaving process quickly.

Illustration 26 (left) pictures a sampler of various patterns achieved with this weave. Descriptions of how to weave each type of pattern are included in the detailed weaving instructions that follow after the preparation and threading of the cards and hints on their turning. Illustration 27 (page 100) shows the lower portion of the front of the sampler, and can

I-26. *Pattern sampler, two-color manipulated weave (5¾" x 9'), by Elfleda Russell*

This sampler, made with fifty cards and three-ply rug yarn, demonstrates just some of the variations of surface pattern available with this simplest threading. How to weave each section is explained in detail in the text and diagrams that follow.

Richard Harper

be compared with Illustration 27a to point out that colors are reversed on the back of this two-sided weave.

The three-dimensional sampler introduced on page 130 was done with this same threading.

You will find it easier to make all the pattern variations across the whole pack at first. As soon as turning feels easy, and the basic pattern principles are understood, try splitting the pack into two or three parts and making different patterns on each section. Details for this process are presented below in the section titled "Weaving a Diamond Shape, Turning Portions of the Pack Separately, and Creating Diagonal Boundaries."

Preparing the Cards. See Diagram 42 (facing) for a life-size pattern for a square card. It can be traced, and a pack of at least twenty-four cards cut from a very thin cardboard "tag," available at stationery stores. Make the holes with a one-hole punch.

You can also buy the cards ready-made at your local craft supply store. The source list (page 176) mentions several mail-order suppliers of cards.

Note the clockwise lettering of the holes, starting at the top left corner, and the numbering of the sides. Number and letter the front and back of each card as shown at *b:*

1. Complete the front face with side 1 at the top.
2. Flip the card sideways so that side 1 remains on top and and corner *x* moves from right to left.
3. With the front face down now, the location of the front numbers would appear as shown if the cards were transparent.
4. Number and letter the back exactly as you did the front, realizing that sides 1 and 3 are the same, but that the remaining sides and all holes carry different marks. (Side 4 shows the 2 on reverse.)

Point *c* indicates that light-colored warps will be passed through the A and B holes, and dark-colored warps through the C and D holes, when the threading process, pictured in detail in Diagram 43 (page 91), begins. Twenty pattern cards are recommended. Four border cards, two for each side, should be

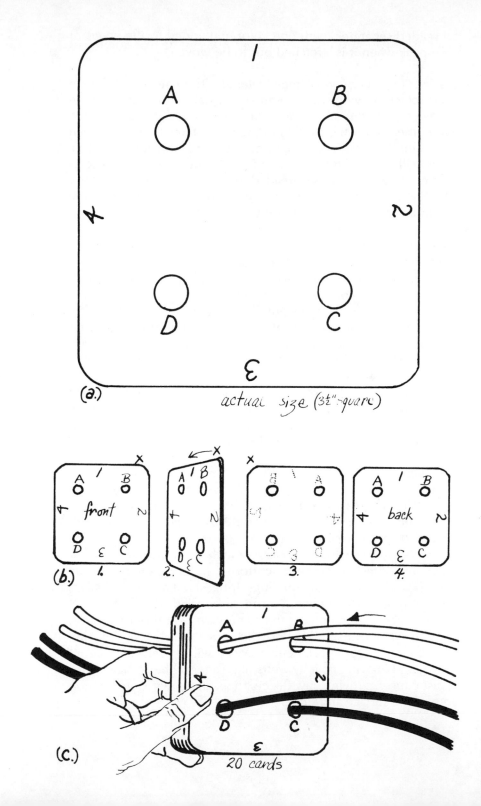

(a.)

actual size (3¼" square)

(b.)

front   back

1.   2.   3.   4.

(c.)

20 cards

threaded separately with one color and added to the edges of the pack when it is stretched out to be woven.

Selecting Warp and Other Materials. The nature of the yarn you select for warp will depend somewhat on the nature of the project. Any smooth, strong yarn will work. The thicker the yarn, the thicker the cloth, and the wider the strip with a given number of cards. For example, twenty cards threaded with rug yarn will weave a two-and-a-half-inch-wide strip, over twice as wide as twenty cards threaded with fine cotton rug warp. Adding cards makes both strips get wider. Colored cotton rug warp and fine pearl cotton are both excellent for belts.

Be sure your warp threads are strong and resist wear, since they must stand up to being stretched taut while weaving and resist the friction of the turning cards. Test them by pulling on them and rubbing your fingernails hard back and forth on the fiber. If it breaks or frays, it is unsuitable for card weaving warp.

Untextured medium-weight yarns are easiest to work with. Most of the samplers presented in this chapter are made with three-ply rug yarn, and it is very comfortable material to use. Beginners may wish to use this yarn, or an equivalent weight in cotton or linen, to start.

If you want to use color, select one very light tone and one very dark tone for good contrast. The sampler of this weave (Illustration 26, page 87) had black and white rug yarn threaded into the two side packs, and black and gray threaded into the center.

Thick and novelty textured yarns can be experimented with after some control is acquired. Heavy ropes and handspun yarns are not easy to work with but can be used to provide a dramatic change of pace as warp. Special larger heavy cardboard or even plywood cards can be made to accommodate extremely heavy yarns, such as one-inch-thick mariner's sisal or jute, and some of the heavy cotton seine lines. Other novelty warps, such as ribbons, trimmings, fringes, raffia (real and fake), plastic tubing, fishing line . . . can all be tried.

The weft is traditionally the same yarn as the border cards. That is what you should start with now, but obviously it, too, can be varied for special effect. More will be said later about using and inlaying novelty wefts like cane, rubber or leather or plastic tubing, roving, raw fleece, rope, sticks, wire, etc., to pop out of the surface and sides.

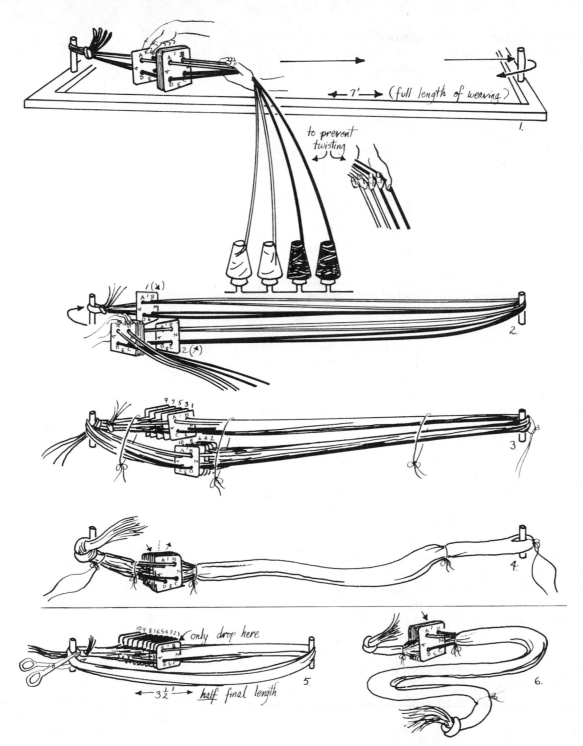

D-43. *Speedy threading for two-color manipulated card weaving*

The fisherman's netting shuttle shown on page 38 is handy to weave with if conventional yarn is used for warp. Knife-edge shuttles, made specifically for card weaving, can be purchased but are not really necessary.

Threading the Cards, Winding Off the Warp. The drawings of Diagram 43 (page 91) picture two variations on a rapid method of warping up the cards for two-color weaving. Any makeshift device can replace the pegs and frame shown here. Both variations require a separate source of yarn for each of the four threads shown carried by the cards in the previous diagram. You need two cones, or fist-sized balls, of the light color and two of the dark. If you don't have pegs to hold the cones, place the four cones or balls in their own separate containers — bags or boxes — on the floor, centered below the devices you will wind the warps around. Students in my soft sculpture classes use long and short working tables to wind onto, taping a stick or any kind of barrier a couple of inches back from the two front ends to keep the warps from slipping off. Since the alternative pictured at 1 through 4 is the quickest method, the very long working tables are grabbed up first. Those stuck with shorter tables do nicely using the second alternative, and save leg work.

In detail, here is the procedure: first, decide how many pattern cards are to be used — here, twenty have been recommended for starting. The four solid-colored border cards will be threaded separately later. Stack the deck of twenty cards all the same way, with side 1 on top.

Pass one light warp end through the A holes, the other light end through the B holes, and the dark ends through the C and D holes respectively. Knot the four ends together, then tie them to the left peg as shown at 1 or to the left leg of a long table.

Hold the feeding warps in your left hand as shown to prevent their twisting, trying to keep that left hand somewhat centered above the yarn sources so it periodically pulls straight up to feed out more warp length. Hold the pack of cards in your right hand and start sliding it toward the right-hand peg or table edge. Approximately a foot in from the starting peg or table edge, drop off the last card of the pack and continue the others on. After circling round the right end, drop off a second card a foot before the left peg, as shown at 2, or at that point underneath the table. Continue to wind the warp off in a circle, dropping at the start, and finish off each loop. Winding off twenty cards requires ten full circles, which finish back at the left. Loop the warps a few times round the left peg — or if you are at the table, cut them with about two feet extra and tie them round the left table leg.

Next, as shown at 3, tie keepers round the warps before and after the cards, at one or two points along the warp length and at the right peg. If you are using the table, tie separate keepers on the warps above and below the table, placing them for now only between the cards and the right end. Then put an elastic round each pack, release the ends from the left table leg and, pulling against the right end, bring both sections together. Stroke the left ends of the warp out, cut them off even, and tie them all into a big knot. As shown at 4, this is easily done on the pegs by releasing the left ends from that peg, and cutting and knotting them while pulling against the right peg.

Finally, attach a very, very strong anchor cord just above that knot, as also seen at 4, and anchor the left knot to something fixed, such as the door hinge or doorknob, seen in Diagram 44 (page 94). Pulling against that anchor, release the keepers, stroke out any slack or twist, and tie this end into a knot.

At 5 and 6 the alternate warping method is shown for winding the warp onto a setup only half the length of the finished work. Here, all cards are dropped at one point on each loop, then the starting end of the loop is cut and both ends of warp knotted.

The upward and downward arrows appearing above the cards indicate the "threading direction" (as viewed from the side of the cards seen in the drawing) that results from the two threading processes. The downward arrow indicates that the warp passes down through the holes to the starting knot (left knot); the upward arrow indicates that they come up through the holes to the starting knot. The importance of this will be discussed shortly. Just notice now that when cards are dropped at two points on the warping circle, half the pack has one threading direction, half the other, whereas the whole pack has the same threading direction when all cards are dropped at one point. The threading direction will be easily adjusted to your weaving needs later so need be of no great concern now.

Make two more balls of one color and warp the four border cards in this same manner.

Add two of them onto either edge of the pack when you

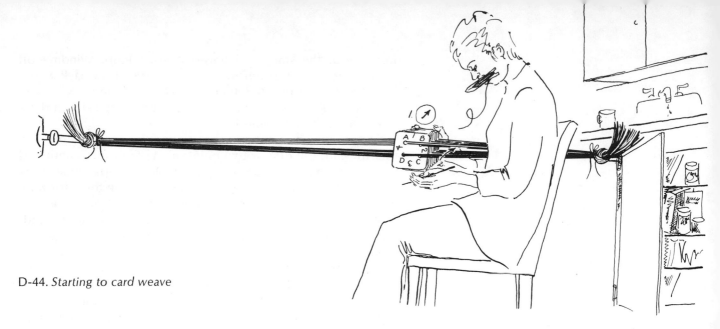

D-44. *Starting to card weave*

stretch them between two fixed points to begin weaving. If a strip of contrasting color is wanted within the pattern cards, as is the case in the pattern sampler, where gray replaced white warp in some center cards, wind that pack separately and insert the contrasting cards into the whole pack also at the tie-up time.

Stretching the Pack Between Two Fixed Points. Two strong new keeper cords can be knotted round all the separately prepared and arranged sections of the complete pack, at either end next to their knots, to hold them all together as you stretch them between two points just prior to weaving.

Diagram 44 (above) shows card weaving stretched between the door hinge of a kitchen cupboard and an opposite door knob. Any two fixed points will do. Although the border cards would actually be included by now, they are not shown here, so as to clearly illustrate the position of the contrasting warps of the pattern cards.

With a shuttle threaded and poised for action, and four sticks (such as thin twigs, pencils, bamboo meat skewers, knitting needles) ready to insert into the first four to six *sheds* to help spread the warps and remove any difference in warp tension, the right-handed weaver sits to the left of the warps at the starting end.

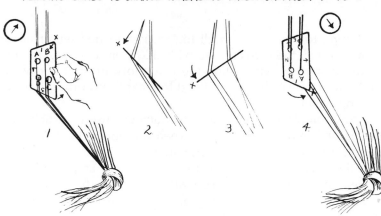

FLIPPING CARDS TO CHANGE THREADING DIRECTION FROM ↗ to ↘

REVERSE PROCESS TO CHANGE FROM ↘ TO ↗

D-45. *Flipping cards to change threading direction*

Before starting, all the cards are set the same way, having side 1 on top and the same threading direction, as described in Diagram 45 (above).

Here, the circled upward arrow (1) indicates the threading direction is upward for all the cards. All downward is optional for starting.

Arrow 2 shows the weaving shed between the two top and two lower warps, made when the cards sit square in the warps.

Adjusting Threading Direction. The total significance of the threading direction is described in the explanation of weaving diagonal stripes, for it is here that absolute control of the threading direction is important. But the beginner is encouraged to start off with shapes and patterns made up of vertical and horizontal lines. In these patterns, different threading directions within the pack are not wanted, as they simply result in unwanted flicks of weft showing at the pivot points, which confuse the pattern.

Depending on which threading process you use, as you now check through the pack you will find either all the cards threaded one way, or some sections of each threading direction. If they aren't all the same, flip each card that is needed to make them all follow the direction of the majority of the cards, using the simple flipping process pictured in Diagram 45. Any flipping that is done in the future must be done when

95

either side 1 or 3 is on top, to keep the same side up after the flip.

Starting to Weave. With all the cards threaded either up or down, and all the cards turned with side 1 on top, you are now ready to start weaving. Slide the cards forward and backward in the warps near the starting end to clear the warps and make turning easier.

Now, referring to Diagram 46 (facing), insert a stick into the natural middle opening between the upper, light A and B threads of side 1 and the lower, dark C and D threads of side 3. Pull the stick as far back to the starting knot as possible and leave it there. *Without squeezing the cards together,* place your thumbs on top of the pack, your fingers on the bottom, and turn the pack one turn forward, or toward the far end, away from you, to bring side 2 to the top. Insert another stick in the middle shed, and pull it down hard against the first one. Turn forward again to bring side 3 up, and again insert a stick. Do the same for side 4. As you weave this sequence, gently encourage the warps to spread slightly apart out of the starting knot, to help the cards quickly find a comfortable spacing that makes turning smooth but does not spread them so wide as to allow the weft to show. If sufficient spreading has occurred by the time side 1 comes up again, and you are satisfied all warps have an equal tension (extra stuffing can be forced under loose warps over the stick-woven section to take out slack), then start your shuttle across this row. Before continuing, here are some hints on turning, and a description of the weaving you just did.

Hints on Turning the Cards and Weaving Neat Edges. Turning the cards becomes easier and faster once the warps are spread and you get the knack of the following: first — how to hold the pack with both hands without squeezing the cards together; second — where the most comfortable place is to apply pressure with thumbs and fingers for both types of turns; third — how to clear the warps as you turn by gently raking the pack forward and back during turning; and finally — clearing the shed by raking the cards right back to the weaving when the turn is complete, then pushing it forward about a foot, taking care to keep the pack square in the warps for maximum shed opening. Just before passing the shuttle through, bend down

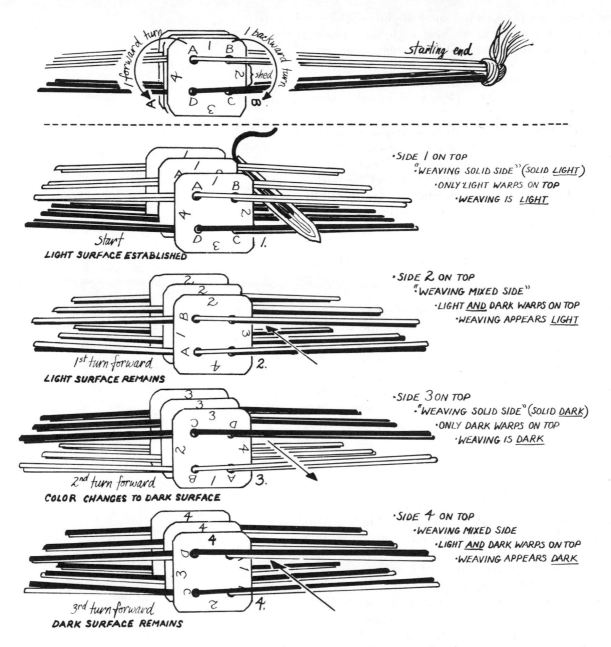

starting end

start
LIGHT SURFACE ESTABLISHED

- SIDE 1 ON TOP
  - "WEAVING SOLID SIDE" (SOLID <u>LIGHT</u>)
  - ONLY LIGHT WARPS ON **TOP**
  - WEAVING IS <u>LIGHT</u>

1st turn forward
LIGHT SURFACE REMAINS

- SIDE 2 ON TOP
  - "WEAVING MIXED SIDE"
    - LIGHT <u>AND</u> DARK WARPS ON TOP
    - WEAVING APPEARS <u>LIGHT</u>

2nd turn forward
COLOR CHANGES TO DARK SURFACE

- SIDE 3 ON TOP
  - "WEAVING SOLID SIDE" (SOLID <u>DARK</u>)
    - ONLY DARK WARPS ON TOP
    - WEAVING IS <u>DARK</u>

3rd turn forward
DARK SURFACE REMAINS

- SIDE 4 ON TOP
  - WEAVING MIXED SIDE
    - LIGHT <u>AND</u> DARK WARPS ON TOP
    - WEAVING APPEARS <u>DARK</u>

D-46. *The solid and mixed sheds of the two-color manipulated weave*

The drawing at the top shows the location of the weaving shed, and what is meant by forward
and backward turning. The lower drawings picture each of the four basic sheds you have to choose
from in order to manipulate all the two-color patterns. The sequence starts with side 1 on
top, then shows three forward turns. A fourth turn forward would bring side 1 to the top again.

and look sideways through the shed, slightly rocking the cards to see if you have them on the best angle for the widest shed. When no warps are questionable in their position above or below the shed, then weave.

Simplified, this is the process: turn the cards, raking slightly; rake the turned pack right back, then forward; check that the shed is clear, and weave.

You will start to notice that neat edges depend on your pulling the weft snug after it has turned back into the weave at each edge. Most weavers leave a loop of weft sticking out at the start of each row, to be pulled snug after the next turn and just prior to weaving. So the insertion of the shuttle is always preceded by a tug on the projecting tail of your weft just to remove that loop at the start of the last row.

The Basic Sheds of the Two-Color Weave and Horizontal Stripes. With side 1 on top for the second time, examine the five rows you have just woven.

Notice that a light horizontal stripe was made with the first two rows of weaving, a dark horizontal stripe was made with the second two rows, and a light stripe has started again with this fifth row, where side 1 is again on top.

Diagram 46 pictures and explains the four types of sheds you have just woven. Notice there that when you continue turning in one direction, a "solid" color side is followed by a "mixed" color side, then solid, then mixed, *the mixed side always opting to show in the weave the color of the solid side that preceded it.*

When "mixed" side 2 follows side 1 in the weaving sequence, it chooses to appear light, even though it carries an equal number of light and dark warp threads.

When mixed side 4 follows solid dark side 3, it chooses to appear dark, even though it too carries an equal number of light threads.

If you make a fourth turn forward to bring up side 1, weave it, then reverse the direction of your turns to make four woven turns backward, or toward you, again ending with side 1 on top, then another set of horizontal stripes is made. Notice that this time the mixed sides change their options because they now follow different solid sides.

Of the four sides you have to work with, two are fixed or can produce only one surface each — solid sides 1 and 3 —

and two are flexible — mixed sides 2 and 4 — and can be persuaded to produce either a light or a dark surface, depending on which of the two solid sides is made to precede them. You will see how all the pattern manipulations that follow operate on this principle.

To summarize then, the turns that revealed the fundamental mechanism underlying two-color pattern weaving produce even, horizontal stripes. Start by weaving with side 1 on top, then continue thereafter with four turns forward and four turns backward as follows:

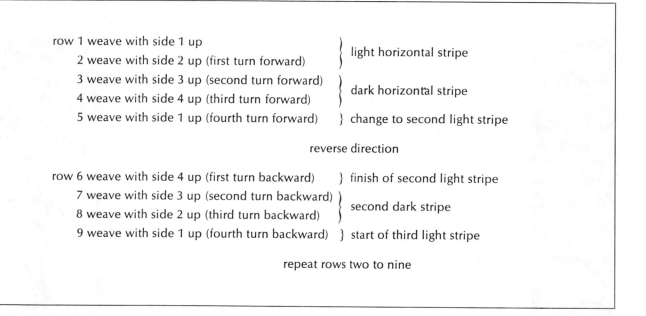

row 1 weave with side 1 up   } light horizontal stripe
    2 weave with side 2 up (first turn forward)

    3 weave with side 3 up (second turn forward)   } dark horizontal stripe
    4 weave with side 4 up (third turn forward)

    5 weave with side 1 up (fourth turn forward)   } change to second light stripe

reverse direction

row 6 weave with side 4 up (first turn backward)   } finish of second light stripe

    7 weave with side 3 up (second turn backward)
    8 weave with side 2 up (third turn backward)   } second dark stripe

    9 weave with side 1 up (fourth turn backward)   } start of third light stripe

repeat rows two to nine

What would happen if you reversed direction after weaving row 4, where side 4 was up, and wove back to side 3, then side 2? If you can see that the dark color, set up when side 3 first came up, would stay on top for the three rows of weaving that follow it, you are getting the idea of how this weave works, and understanding that a color can be sustained in this manner leads you nicely into the next pattern principle.

Rocking Around the Solid Sides to Sustain Colors. As you

Photographs by Richard Harper

pattern textures

I-27. *Lower detail of pattern sampler of two-color manipulated weave*

The cards can be realigned at any time in order to orchestrate changing patterns. The names of the design elements included in this portion of the sampler accompany the illustration.

diamonds

diagonal boundaries

diagonal stripes

working portions
of pack separately

vertical stripes

sustaining a color

checks

horizontal stripes

I-27a. *Reverse face of lower detail of two-color manipulated weave sampler*

Colors are reversed on the back of this weave. Notice that the locations of smooth and jagged diagonal stripes are also reversed.

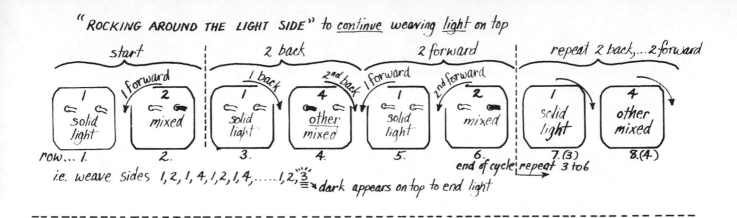

"ROCKING AROUND THE LIGHT SIDE" to <u>continue</u> weaving <u>light</u> on top

i.e. weave sides 1, 2, 1, 4, 1, 2, 1, 4, ... 1, 2, <u>3</u> ᷄ dark appears on top to end light

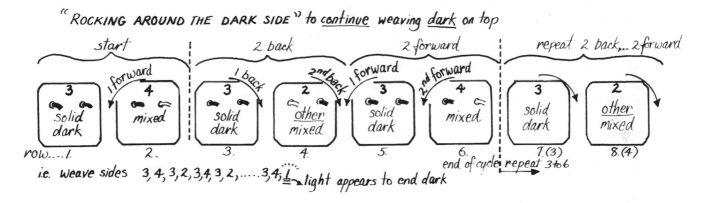

"ROCKING AROUND THE DARK SIDE" to <u>continue</u> weaving <u>dark</u> on top

i.e. weave sides 3, 4, 3, 2, 3, 4, 3, 2, ... 3, 4, <u>1</u> ᷄ light appears to end dark

D-47. *Rocking around solid sides to sustain colors*

now know, then, this flexibility of sides 2 and 4 allows you to sustain the light or dark color on the surface of the weave. Diagram 47 (above) explains how you can continue a color as long as you want with a rocking sequence just implied with the sustained dark stripe.

After completing at least two sets of horizontal stripes, and returning to side 1 on top, you could begin the sequence *rocking around the light side* to sustain the light surface for a short distance.

Notice in the drawing that after the two starting rows you continue a two-turns-forward, two-turns-backward rocking motion, weaving every turn, that has you weaving side 1, then one mixed side (2), then back to side 1 again, followed by the other mixed side (4).

Rocking around the dark side is the same process, with side 1 replaced by side 3 in the middle of the rocking sequence.

Weaving Checks. To prepare to weave checks, adjust the pattern cards so that the first two cards have side 1 on top, the next two have side 3 on top, the next two side 1 . . . all across the pattern pack. Instead of two cards per group, there can be more per group, to make wider checks. Checks of different sizes can be combined, too, by making a symmetrical or random change in the alternating groups of cards.

Diagram 53 (page 109) includes motifs made up of different-sized checks. The first part of the sampler in Illustration 27 (page 100) starts with even checks across the pack.

When the card groups are adjusted, make the same turning and weaving sequence as you did at the start for horizontal stripes. That is, four turns forward, four backward. This sequence prevents the accumulation of twists in the warp beyond the cards. A series of turns in one direction would also make checks, but builds up twists. A description of a remedy for twists that do build up can be found on page 113.

Longer checks are made by reverting to the rocking around a solid side sequence.

Shorter checks are made by continuing the four forward, four backward turning sequence, but only weaving the sheds of the solid sides. In other words, skip weaving the mixed sheds.

Weaving Vertical Stripes. If you continue the rocking around a solid side sequence long enough, the elongated checks become vertical sripes. This was done with center checks in the pattern sampler, page 100. So the process is: align for checks, then rock around solid sides.

Changing Colors. Whenever solid sides come to the top, you can adjust any cards two turns in either direction to bring the other solid side up, prior to weaving the original solid row.

Test which turning direction is best. The one opposite to the direction you last turned should prevent an unwanted extra twist in the warps.

Knowing that you can change color at will, with any portion of the pack, is the key to designing and orchestrating different areas within the continuing weave.

Working Sections of the Pack Differently. In the gray center section of the lower portion of Illustration 27 checks were sustained into vertical stripes by turning this center portion

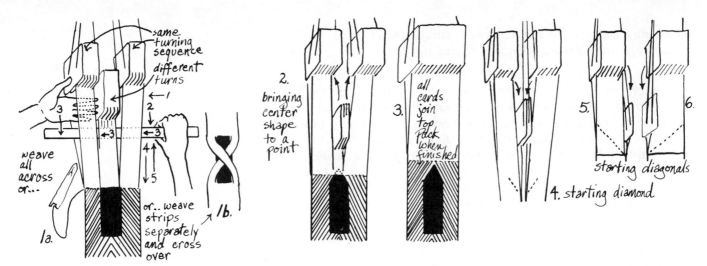

D-48. *Turning portions of the pack separately and creating diagonal boundaries*

The text describes these processes in detail on pages 104 to 105. Realize that these basic diagonals can occur anywhere, and they needn't be symmetrical. Once you can weave diagonals, as well as vertical and horizontal stripes, you can weave all letters and numbers, as well as motifs that are abstract or an image.

of the pack to rock around a solid side while the remaining side packs continue making checks. After a short distance, the two center light stripes were changed to dark by the method just described, and the dark rectangle was then sustained.

Cards producing different kinds of areas, like this rectangle within a checkerboard, are most easily kept track of when their positions in the warp are staggered.

Part 1 of Diagram 48 (above) shows the pack split in three as is needed for the turning of this part of the sampler. This same division of cards is necessary when a very thick pack of cards is too difficult to turn all at once. In fact, this three-way split was needed throughout this fifty-card sampler, with further subdivision being made wherever multiple splits in the design dictated.

Although the shuttle weaves across the whole pack when this segregation is used to create contrasting pattern areas, this is a good time to mention that these divisions of the pack could also be woven separately to form three strips, say six to eight inches long. These separate strips can then be crossed by making the two outside packs change places, or these strips can be twisted, as described with the three-dimensional sampler (page 130).

Weaving a Diamond Shape, Turning Portions of the Pack Separately, and Creating Diagonal Boundaries

1. See the diagram on page 103. The three packs are turned separately, each making the sequence required by the design, and each in turn ending in a forward rake that has the center pack finish behind the side packs. Following the numbers and directions of the arrows, insert a shed stick (ruler) flat, from the right, just under that pack at 1, then slide it down, 2, to just below the center pack, where you next push it across that shed and the left shed, which is passed down by your left hand, 3. Then pull the shed stick back to the weaving, 4, then forward to the center pack, 5, and turn it on edge. Weave the shuttle just under the stick. This triple-shedding becomes rapid with a little practice.

2. *Inward-sloping diagonal boundaries* are seen in Illustration 27 (page 100), where the dark sides slope in to follow diagonal stripes, and also make the tops of solid diamonds. They are seen in this drawing sloping in the sides of the center dark rectangle to a top point. Each of these examples is made with the pack split in three, continuing the turning required of each area and passing a pair of edge cards from the center pack up to each side pack after each solid side comes up (every second turn) but before it is woven. Turn the adjusted cards up to the side required to blend them into the design being carried on in the side packs they have just joined, then weave. The center pack thus gets two cards narrower following every second turn. This means the center pack should start with an even number of cards, and the sequence obviously ends when the center pack runs out.

3. All the cards can again be turned together at any time to make a section of pattern flash across the whole surface. A dark horizontal stripe is made here after the center section comes to a point. The cards can again be segregated if you plan more splits in the design.

4. To begin a white diamond, or any expanding shape in the center of a dark field (see the diamonds in Illustration 27), bring down the two center cards of the pack and turn each one the opposite way for two turns, to bring up side 1. On this first pair, you will have to experiment to find which turns (opposite for each) make the dark threads on each card twist round to the outside of the light diamond. Continue that direc-

tion of turn on each card brought down to that same side while the diamond expands. This means the left card turns two forward, the right two back, or vice versa, to make smooth-edged expanding diagonal boundaries. Weave that row (a solid side row) and then on all the pack continue the rocking sequence required to sustain the dark background and light diamond, not breaking the sequence. This will be one turn, either forward or back, to a mixed side. Weave that, then turn back to the solid sides and, before weaving, bring down one more card from each side pack, bringing up side 1 with the appropriate turns of each adjusted card, to have now four cards in the center. Then weave. Continue repeating this sequence. Always adjust before weaving each solid side, weaving the alternating mixed sides normally with both packs turned together. When the top of the diamond is to start sloping in to the center, follow the procedure for inward sloping boundaries, being sure that you change the direction of the adjustment turns to keep the edges smooth. So, on the lower part of the diamond, the side at which cards were turning forward when adjusted now has them turn back.

5. A diagonal starts at the right edge by gradually adding to a single card brought down on that side to contrast with the background.

6. A diagonal starts at the left when opposing cards gradually accumulate on that side. A pause in the accumulation of contrasting cards, while the rocking around a solid side sequence continues, makes the borders temporarily run straight.

Weaving Diagonal Stripes. Illustration 27 (page 100) shows that you have the choice of weaving diagonal stripes that are smooth or jagged. The back view of this section of weave, Illustration 27a (page 100), shows that where diagonals are smooth on the front they are jagged on the back, and vice versa.

The type of diagonal you get on the front depends on the relationship you establish between the threading direction and the sequential alignment of the cards' sides, which causes diagonal stripes. This relationship can be altered anytime.

To line the cards up so they produce diagonal stripes, turn the left-hand pattern card with side 1 on top, the second with side 2, the third with 3, the fourth with 4, and repeat across the pack. Reading the pack from left to right you can now say that the sides are aligned in ascending order.

Smooth diagonal stripes result if the threading direction is the same — that is, ascending. Be sure to read the threading direction from the left also. When ascending, the threads come *up* out of the holes toward the starting knot.

Jagged stripes can be made with this same ascending alignment of the sides, left to right, if the threading direction is downward or opposing the direction of the alignment. This means that, still reading from the left, the warps go down through the holes toward the starting knot.

Note that a descending alignment of the sides (4,3,2,1,4 . . .) couples with a downward threading direction to produce smooth stripes and with an upward threading direction to produce jagged stripes. The only difference from the first alignment is that the stripes slope in the opposite directions with forward and backward turns. Continuing to turn in one direction makes the stripes continue sloping one way, reversing the turns makes them slope on the opposite angle.

Diagram 49 (right) shows a pack of pattern cards split in half, with the left half, *a,* threaded downward to correlate with a descending alignment of the sides, which starts 4,3,2,1,4 . . . to the middle card. Threading direction is changed by the flips pictured in Diagram 45 (page 95). Whatever side that left middle card has on top, the first middle card of the right half, *b,* repeats. Pack *b* then continues in an ascending alignment of the sides to the last edge card, which will be the same as the edge card of the left pack. Notice the border cards aren't shown for clarity; they can continue the sequence they are adjacent to, so reading the pack is easier. The threading direction of the right half is adjusted upward to correlate with the ascending side alignment.

If the downward threading direction continued right across the pack, the right-hand half of the diagonal stripes would weave jagged. If the threading directions were both reversed, all jagged stripes would result.

Diagram 50 (right) shows the turning sequence for this alignment that results in the V's and diamonds pictured there.

Making Patterns and Designs from Diagonal Stripes. A great variety of patterns and designs can be achieved by making one or more pivot points across the pack. As already suggested in Diagram 50, a pivot point marks a change in the direction of the alignment of the sides and/or the threading direction,

D-49. *Correlating alignment of sides with threading direction to weave smooth V's and diamonds*

Pictured here is one central pivot point in the sequential alignment of sides that makes diagonal stripes turn into the V's and diamonds pattern in Diagram 50.

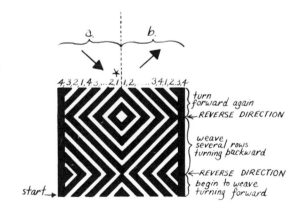

D-50. *V's and diamond pattern made with one central pivot point in the sequential alignment of sides, plus threading direction*

Turning a few rows forward, then back, then forward again, makes the setup pictured in Diagram 49 automatically produce this pattern.

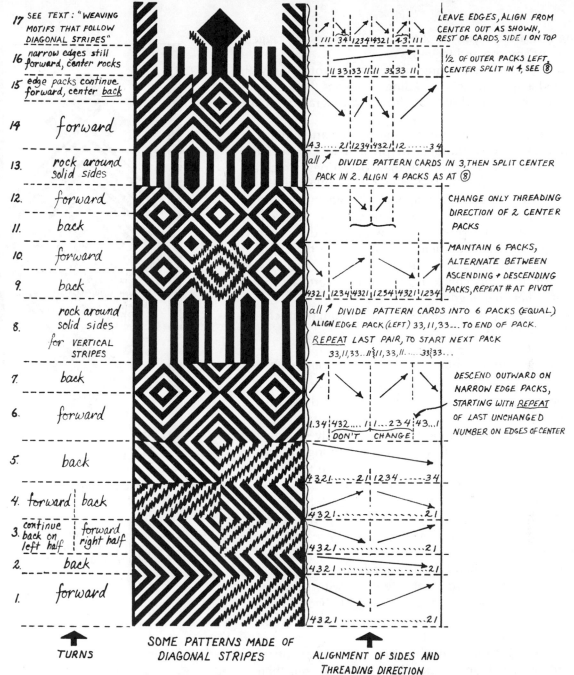

TURNS (left column, numbered):

17 — SEE TEXT: "WEAVING MOTIFS THAT FOLLOW DIAGONAL STRIPES"
16 — narrow edges still forward, center rocks
15 — edge packs continue forward, center back
14 — forward
13 — rock around solid sides
12 — forward
11 — back
10 — forward
9 — back
8 — rock around solid sides for VERTICAL STRIPES
7 — back
6 — forward
5 — back
4 — forward | back
3 — continue back on left half | forward right half
2 — back
1 — forward

TURNS

SOME PATTERNS MADE OF DIAGONAL STRIPES

ALIGNMENT OF SIDES AND THREADING DIRECTION (right column):

LEAVE EDGES, ALIGN FROM CENTER OUT AS SHOWN, REST OF CARDS, SIDE 1 ON TOP
/// 34 1234 432/ 43 ///

½ OF OUTER PACKS LEFT, CENTER SPLIT IN 4, SEE ⑧
// 33 33 // // 33 33 //

43.....21 1234 432/ 12.....34

DIVIDE PATTERN CARDS IN 3, THEN SPLIT CENTER PACK IN 2. ALIGN 4 PACKS AS AT ⑧

all ↗ CHANGE ONLY THREADING DIRECTION OF 2 CENTER PACKS

MAINTAIN 6 PACKS, ALTERNATE BETWEEN ASCENDING + DESCENDING PACKS, REPEAT # AT PIVOT
4321 1234 432/ 1234 432/ 1234

all ↗ DIVIDE PATTERN CARDS INTO 6 PACKS (EQUAL) ALIGN EDGE PACK (LEFT) 33,11,33... TO END OF PACK. REPEAT LAST PAIR, TO START NEXT PACK
33,11,33...// // 11,33,11....33 33...

DESCEND OUTWARD ON NARROW EDGE PACKS, STARTING WITH REPEAT OF LAST UNCHANGED NUMBER ON EDGES OF CENTER
1.34 432.....// ...234 43...1
DON'T CHANGE

4321.....21 1234.....34

4321.................21

4321.................21

4321.................21

4321.................21

ALIGNMENT OF SIDES AND THREADING DIRECTION

D-51. *Some patterns made of diagonal stripes having various pivot points*

Pictured here are just a few of the multitude of patterns and designs that can be built of smooth and jagged diagonal stripes when a variety of pivot points is set up. Notice how the diamond patterns can be extended vertically by realigning and weaving for vertical stripes, as described in the text (page 102). This chart shows that you can change the alignment and threading direction at any time, and that solid, sustained color areas can fill in anywhere (see diagonal boundaries) so that highly controlled designs and motifs can result.

depending on whether you want all smooth stripes, all jagged, or a mixture of smooth and jagged.

Diagram 49 (page 106) pictures one central pivot point, with the correlated alignment and threading directions that will produce the smooth diamond pattern shown in Diagram 50 (page 106).

Diagram 51 (page 107) pictures some of the variety that can be achieved by various numbers of pivot points. It includes the vertical extension of sections of diagonal stripes, which are created by realigning for vertical stripes that reflect the final position of the dark and light diagonals. To do this, pause at any point in the turning, and adjust the cards to have either side 3 up or side 1 up, depending on whether a dark or light diagonal stripe ends directly below. Make all the threading in the same direction and use the rocking around a solid side sequence to extend this check alignment into vertical stripes. Return to any diagonal alignment at any time.

Diagram 52 (right) is presented a little tongue-in-cheek, to suggest three things:

1. Reflected images can be implied by smooth and jagged diagonals.

2. The dark color (black here) can be threaded as usual into the C and D holes of all the cards, whereas the A and B holes can be threaded with continually changing pastel shades, which will cause a shimmering appearance in the areas where light is on top. Here the shimmer is the sun setting on the Old South!

   If one light shade is threaded into every A hole, and another shade into every B hole, meshed horizontal stripes will be produced when you weave to rock around the light side.

   If, on the other hand, both threads are the same in one or a group of cards that alternates with single or groups of cards carrying a different light shade in the A and B holes, then vertical stripes will result when rocking around the light side.

   Consider threading half the pack with one shade of light threads, half the pack with another shade, then shuffling the pack before starting to weave to produce a random shimmer.

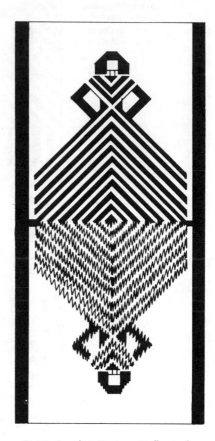

D-52. Scarlet O'Hara Reflected at Sunset (*smooth and jagged diagonal stripes*)

This drawing of smooth and jagged diagonal stripes is presented rather facetiously to bring up further possibilities for diagonal stripes.

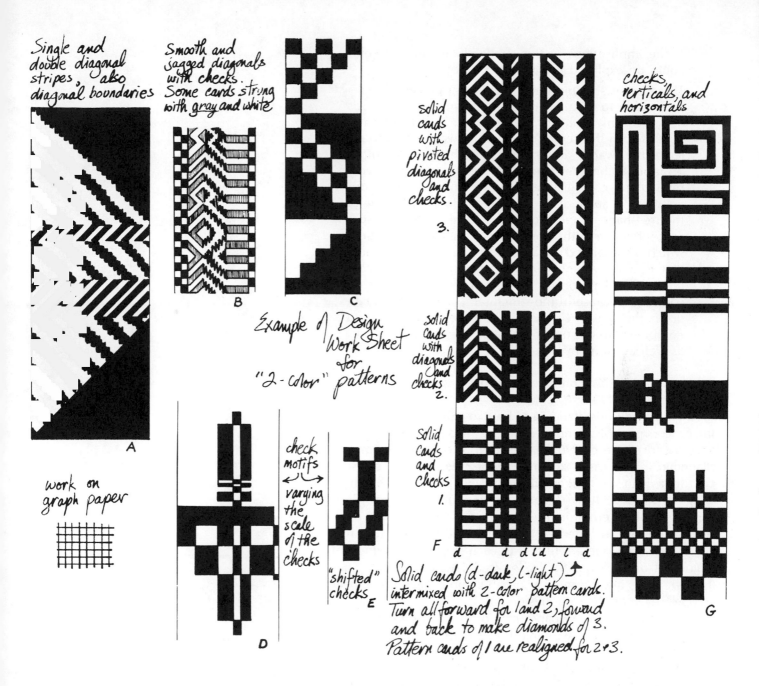

Single and double diagonal stripes, also diagonal boundaries

Smooth and jagged diagonals with checks. Some cards strung with gray and white

checks, verticals, and horizontals

Solid cards with pivoted diagonals and checks.

3.

Solid cards with diagonals and checks.

2.

Solid cards and checks

1.

Example of Design Work Sheet for "2-color" patterns

work on graph paper

check motifs ↔ varying the scale of the checks

"shifted" checks

A

B

C

D

E

F

G

d   d   d l d   l   d

Solid cards (d-dark, l-light) intermixed with 2-color pattern cards. Turn all forward for 1 and 2, forward and back to make diamonds of 3. Pattern cards of 1 are realigned for 2 + 3.

D-53. *Example of design work sheet for two-color patterns*

The implications of this subtle change in one color could be explored extensively, no doubt.

3. Threading is so rapid for the two-color process that it's reasonable to consider threading a large pack of cards to weave only a short motif, such as *Scarlet Reflected at Sunset,* in the center of very long warps, then to release the warps and commence shaping the other off-loom techniques above and below, trapping a very refined image, or just fragment, within the organic convolutions of some off-loom shaping, done with some of the free-hanging techniques. Since this is the first specific reference to the possibility of such a combination, which is elaborated on later, it could be mentioned now that double twining is a free-hanging, off-loom technique that harmonizes exceptionally well with card weaving, because of the structural relationship brought up at the outset. In choosing off-loom techniques to combine with this one, thought can be given to contrast as well as harmony.

For more of this combined approach, see "Card Tricks," starting on page 140.

As increased understanding of how to manipulate this weaving process possibly stimulates ideas for images or other motifs, a desire for more control may lead you to some preliminary planning. In this case, sketches can be freehand, or very specific ideas can be worked out on graph paper, as shown in Diagram 53 (page 109). The only design found there that is not explained fully there or in the text is part A, where double diagonal stripes are included. You may be able to guess that two cards instead of one are turned to each step in the sequential alignment of the sides (i.e., sides read 1,1,2,2,3,3,4,4 . . . not 1,2,3,4). Turns are the same as usual. Double diagonals appear stepped, even on the smooth side.

The thinking done on paper may or may not be copied exactly into a particular weaving, but it definitely can result in your striving to achieve an unusual effect you may not have thought of otherwise. The kind of free exploration one can do directly with the weaving should dominate your experimenting at first, though, so that its natural tendencies become very familiar. The spontaneous decision-making that can be done with

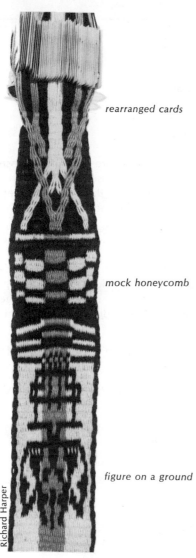

rearranged cards

mock honeycomb

figure on a ground

Richard Harper

I-28. *Upper detail of pattern sampler of two-color manipulated weave*

the figure-on-a-ground process described below is an excellent way to explore the medium directly for motifs.

Weaving Pattern Textures. The three lengths of texture above the diamond section of the pattern sampler depicted in Illustration 27 (page 100) are experiments in novel alignments of the cards, to see what overall textures would result with various forward and backward turning sequences.

The right-hand texture is the now familiar diagonal alignment with three pivot points.

The center has a 3,1,3,1 alignment; the left side a 2,1,2,1 alignment.

Creating a Figure on a Ground. In the lower portion of Illustration 28 (left), the whole pack rocks around a solid side (see pages 99 to 100) to make a light or dark background, and individual or groups of cards are changed to the contrasting color (see page 102) whenever the solid sides come to the top, to create a figure or motif on the background. The contrasting cards, once changed, follow the same turning sequence as the background, so the whole pack can be rocked together. A handy way to keep track of the location of the figure cards is to push them just forward of the background pack, as already discussed with Diagram 48 (page 103).

The contrasting figure color disappears the same way it appears, with two turns prior to the weaving of any solid row.

A symmetrical or nonsymmetrical figure can follow a preplanned design, as suggested with the previous diagram, or it can develop spontaneously if you make adjustment decisions before weaving each solid row.

On the next page is the process for weaving a dark figure on a light background, as seen in the sampler on the left. To make a light figure on a dark background, just exchange sides 1 and 3 below.

Weaving a Mock Honeycomb. The staggered lozenge pattern in the middle of Illustration 28 is called *mock honeycomb* because of its similarity to the honeycomb pattern woven on a four-harness loom.

The cards are aligned as if to weave wide checks. Weave the solid row set up by the alignment, then weave a complete sequence of rocking around a solid side, i.e., weave 1,2,1,4,1,

start light background	row	1 ⎞	turn the whole pack to side 1 and weave
	row	2 ⎛	turn the whole pack one forward to side 2 and weave
	row	3 ⎨	turn the whole pack one back to side 1 and weave
	row	4 ⎠	turn the whole pack one back to side 4 and weave

start figure — row 5 turn the whole pack one forward to side 1, but before weaving choose which cards will start the bottom of the figure, turn those cards two turns backward to bring side 3 to the top, then weave all the pack together, weaving side 1 of the background cards and side 3 of the figure cards

sustain figure — row 6 turn the whole pack one forward (side 2 is up on background cards, side 4 is up on figure cards), and weave

adjust figure — row 7 turn the whole pack one back to solid sides and decide which figure cards to keep longer, which new ones to add, which previous ones to stop. Those that are to start and end now are all turned two forward to change their colors. Those being kept aren't touched. After adjusting, weave this solid row of the whole pack

sustain figure — row 8 turn the whole pack one back (to mixed side 4 on the background cards, mixed side 2 on the figure cards) and weave

adjust figure — row 9 turn the whole pack one forward to solid sides and again make adjustments as at 7, prior to weaving that solid row

— row 10 repeat rows 6 through 9 until the figure is complete and end with rows 2 through 4 for solid light background at the top

turning only those cards set up to weave light checks. This causes the light checks to build for five rows while the dark checks don't grow past the first solid row, the extra wefts passing five times through the first shed made when side 3 was brought up.

After sustaining the light checks for five rows you end having woven side 1. Now turn all the cards two turns forward to change the colors of the checks before weaving. Skip weaving the mixed shed.

Now weave that solid row, and sustain the light checks as before in their new position now. Repeat.

D-54. *Rearranging cards in the pack*

Rearranging Cards. See the upper portion of Illustration 28 (page 111). This process is similar to building a figure on a ground, with the difference being that the contrasting figure cards are lifted right up and out of the pack and inserted at a different spot, after turning to the solid rows but prior to weaving them. Diagram 54 (left) pictures light figure cards with side 1 up (background, side 3 up) being moved a few cards out to the side. This shift causes the figure stripes to jump up and over the surface a short distance. If the rearranged cards are sustained there for one rocking sequence, then jumped again, they produce a stepped, relief diagonal.

So working this technique, continue the rocking around the solid side sequence, pausing before weaving each solid row to decide what stripes should be shifted, and where, what new stripes can start, and old stripes stop.

Notice how the edges of the weaving are affected by the arrival of stripes that originated in the center.

Check the back to decide whether you want to bring that surface to the front by making some shifts below the pack. The back of the rearranged section of this sampler is seen on page 100. The bell hanging in Illustration 29 (page 116) shows the possibility of rearranging portions of threaded-in patterns, the system following next.

Rearranging and Separating Portions of the Pack. See Diagram 55 (page 114). Dedicated to Peter Collingwood, this departure is frankly inspired by his "Macrogauze" technique. The on-loom process he invented involves rearranging small groups of warps threaded into one-inch sections of a cut-up rigid *heddle* (an alternating slot-hole device warps are threaded through that is raised and lowered to make a shed; see Diagram 73, page 140, for a rigid heddle). Card weaving is a natural for this process, since each card can move independently of the others — and carries the potential to make pattern that the rigid heddle lacks.

Groups of cards can begin being rearranged within the pack as just described, then take off on their own, so that the original pack divides up into a network of narrow packs that continually join and separate.

The source weaving in Diagram 55 is shown dark, to clearly contrast with the light strips that spring from it.

Don't forget that, as the network builds, you still have the

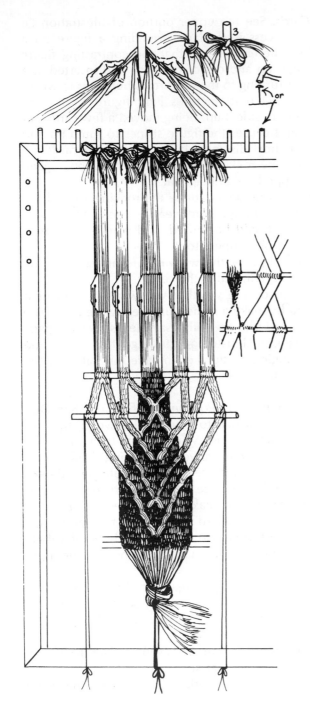

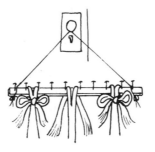

D-55. *Rearranging and separating portions of the pack*

opportunity to use all the card weaving variations presented in this chapter.

Although this network is shown beginning from a single pack here, it could just as well begin from a series of small packs already separated. See "Branched Card Weaving" (page 145) and Diagram 77 (page 146) for a simply woven variation of this.

This process could be sustained through a whole project or could be considered the start of some project incorporating the other off-loom techniques in a sort of variation of the off-loom working process. In the latter case, some cards can continue weaving while others are slipped off at various points, their warps released, then shaped with any of the other off-loom techniques or threaded through a rigid heddle to commence any sort of weaving, perhaps tapestry or pile.

Although a large pegged frame is very handy to work with (and inexpensive to make) you can easily make do by tying both ends to a long stick, carrying large nails at intervals of two or three inches, as pictured to the side of Diagram 55. These sticks can then be tied to your doorknobs or other fixed points when you stretch out the threaded cards to begin work.

Notice as well in this diagram that rods must be inserted into the sheds where new joining of packs occur, to keep the network spread. A few rows of weft, which travel back and forth across all of each new joined pack, should precede and follow each rod. A temporary tack can help keep each section in place on the dowel until the card weaving is complete.

finishing end.

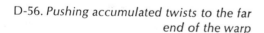

D-56. *Pushing accumulated twists to the far end of the warp*

Collecting Accumulated Twists at the Far End. It won't be long before you notice that an uneven number of turns forward and backward in any card weaving results in a gradual accumulation of twists in the warp beyond the cards. When these start interfering with your turning, work them to the far end and catch them there with a tie.

Just rake a finger up between each two adjacent threads, for the greatest efficiency (see Diagram 56, page 115). Gather the twists on a stick or in your other hand, till a tie holds them at the top.

This should only be necessary once or twice in the process of weaving a ten-foot length. In between, pull groups of cards apart and push their twists ahead a little, every once in a while.

Threaded-In Patterns

When different shades of yarn are threaded into the four holes of each card according to a preplanned draft, simple turning sequences of the whole pack bring the different colors to the top at different points, automatically producing intricate repeat patterns.

Threading doesn't take much longer than in the two-color system, and weaving can be automatic and very fast. Two hours of work can produce a belt, for instance. Although the threaded pattern changes with different turning sequences, it always dominates the surface, not allowing the variety of surface available with the two-color weave but offering great richness and speed in return.

Traditionally, the cards are turned square in the warp, as has been the case thus far, and the turning sequence is a simple rocking motion of four turns forward, four turns backward — repeated throughout, weaving every row, of course. Or — weave sides 1,2,3,4/3,2,1,4/1,2,3,4/ repeat, always pivoting back in the opposite direction following the weaving of side 4. This weaving process is so simple and automatic that no thinking is required. The portability of the strung cards allows you to take them outside with you and string them between trees. An hour and a half can see a whole strip complete. A few afternoons can result in a good tan and enough strips for a very dramatic rug or hanging, or belts for all your lucky friends.

Using any of the drafts that follow, along with this simple turning sequence, will produce attractive results.

Adventuresome weavers may soon grow impatient with this repetitive weaving and the familiarity of the diamond-based motifs that usually result. "Turning Sequences to Try" (page

I-29. *Belts and bell hanging made using threaded-in patterns (courtesy of Diane Becker)*

The belt at left departs from the customary symmetry, and the bell hanging had cards rearranged in the pack to alter the location of sections of pattern and create raised areas, as described with the diagram (54) and text on page 113.

Beads, bells, bones — any objects at all can be strung onto the weft or carried on an inlay cord.

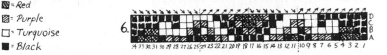

D-57. *Six drafts for threaded-in patterns*

- ■ = Dark
- ▨ = Medium
- □ = Light

Choose any three colors, one dark, one medium, one light, to weave these patterns. Pattern 1 is explored in the sampler in Illustration 30. Pattern 6 indicates the four colors that were used in the sampler in Illustration 31 (page 118), which is pictured in color on the back cover.

- ▨ = Red
- ▧ = Purple
- □ = Turquoise
- ■ = Black

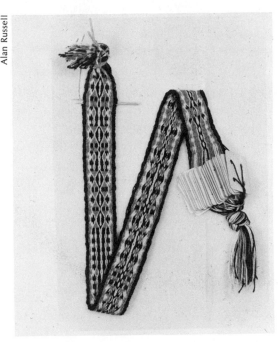

Alan Russell

I-30. *Sampler of draft 1 of Diagram 57*

Each of the turning sequences suggested on pages 121 to 122 has been used here. The definite diamond sections were woven with the 1,2,3,4/3,2,1,4/(repeat) basic sequence. The various vertical sections result from rocking around each of the four sides. The slightly wider undulating pattern of the center part was done with a 1/2,3,4/3,2,1/2,3,4/3,2,1/(repeat) sequence. The left and right sections show the smooth side of the weave; the center shows the diffuse side.

121) lists a number of turning variations that can greatly alter the basic pattern. Rearranging cards, and applying any of the methods described with three-dimensional card weaving and card tricks, can produce further variety. Soon you will want to plan your own designs — it's easy and more fun.

Reading and Designing Pattern Drafts. Diagram 57 (above) presents six pattern drafts that can have any combination of strongly contrasting colors applied. Suitable yarns are the same as those described at the beginning of card weaving (page 90).

The draft is prepared on graph paper. Notice in Diagram 57 that the height of each draft corresponds to the four holes of the square cards, and the length of the draft corresponds to the number of cards in the pack.

The squares are then shaded in to make any pattern pleasing to the eye. It is optional to make the design symmetrical or not; however, the beginner may find symmetry an aid in detecting threading or weaving errors.

With experience, one comes to sense what the draft will basically provide, although there are always surprises when the experimental weaving commences.

Diagonals in the draft produce the greatest variety in the thread combinations that rise with the four sheds, so they are usually used extensively. These diagonals produce diamond motifs on pivoted sequences, hence the predominance of that shape in threaded-in patterns.

If you hold a mirror to the top edge of the draft, so that you see its reflection, you get an idea of the appearance of one basic pivoted sequence in the weaving.

117

The draft itself represents the appearance of the full width of the card weaving for the length of four rows. The pattern can be extended on paper to get the suggestion of woven sequences. Exchange 1,2,3,4 for the letters A,B,C,D at the side, and write out any sequence of turns, realizing that these numbers now represent the side of the cards to be on top of the shed when you weave. List the turning sequence vertically on graph paper, then fill in the horizontal line from the draft that corresponds to each number (i.e., beside 1, fill in the horizontal line of A in the draft). This paper extension can give a fairly good idea of how the draft will appear when woven. However, it's unable to picture truly the actual woven pattern because of the effect of the warp twist on the look of the weaving, so experimenting by weaving is really best.

To understand the relationship between the draft and threaded cards, look again at Diagram 57 and cover all but the far right-hand vertical line of the graph above 1 in sampler draft 1. These four squares represent the four holes of card 1. The letters to the right indicate that the bottom square is hole A, on up to the top square, which is hole D. The shading of each square tells you what color of warp yarn to thread into that hole of card 1. The arrow at the top indicates the threading direction (downward) for all the warps of card 1. As is described with the threading process, this is the direction in which the warps emerge from the front, or upper, marked face to the knot. Only one face of the cards is marked and read for threaded-in pattern weaving.

Since there are two solid-colored border cards on either edge of the sampler draft, you thread each hole of cards 1 and 2 downward with the dark color. Card 3 is solid medium color in this particular design with the threading direction changed to upward. Looking across the line of arrows, you will notice that they change direction not only at the inside of the borders but also at every pivot point across the draft where symmetry occurs in the design. When you make up your own draft, remember to draw the threading direction arrows with a change in direction at each symmetrical pivot in the design. This is a good aspect of the design process to experiment with later, because changes in threading direction greatly alter the appearance of any given pattern draft.

Threading the Cards. This process is done quickly by winding

Alan Russell

I-31. *Sampler of draft 6 of Diagram 57*

Different turning sequences again produce rich changes in the pattern. Two-thirds of the way up in the left section, a center portion of the pack was split to make a series of inward and outward twists described with three-dimensional card weaving.

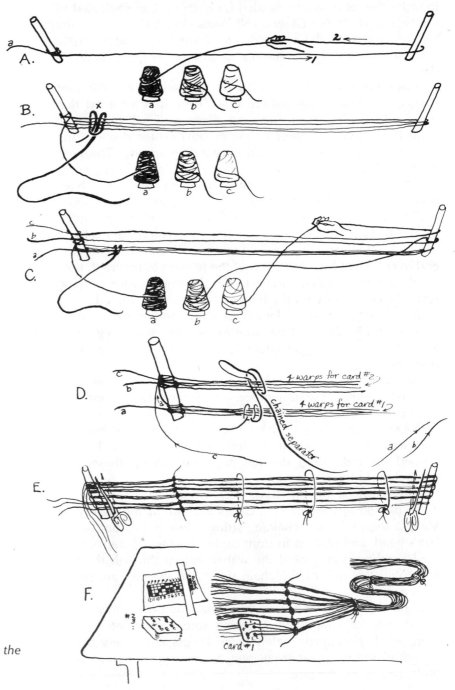

A.

B.

C.

D. 4 warps for card #2
4 warps for card #1
chained separator

E.

F. #2
3
card #1

D-58. *Winding off the warp and threading the cards for threaded-in patterns* in order the set of warps needed for each card, as indicated in the pattern draft. See Diagram 58 (page 119). A chain keeps the sets separated till the cut ends are through their appropriate cards and tied into the starting knot. Here is the process in detail:

Select the colors that are to be applied to the different shaded sections of the pattern draft. Here it is assumed that three colors, a,b,c, are to be used. Place each ball or cone of color in its own container (a bag or box) centered under the pegs or other devices you will be winding around. The pegs are placed apart the distance equal to the length of the project plus three feet. (Eight to nine feet is recommended if you have no definite plans.) Read the four vertical squares above card 1 in the draft to see how many threads of each color are needed for this first card. Here it is assumed a solid dark border is to be woven, so that card 1 will need four darks threads (a). Loop the end of color a at least twice round the left peg to secure it, then wind off two complete circles to get the four threads of dark. Again loop twice round the left peg to secure the thread.

Cut about a two-foot length of string and mount it onto these four threads about one foot to the right of the peg, using a reverse lark's head (Diagram 7, page 37) made so there is only one long tail.

Next, check the squares above card 2 to see what is required for them. Here it is assumed one a is needed, two b, and one c, so color b is started at the left peg and ended at the right with two security loops. Color c starts at the left and makes a full circle to end back at the left peg. Color a can then be looped up and round the left peg again above these, and taken then to the right peg.

When all four threads have been wound for card 2, color c has paused at the left peg, colors a and b at the right peg. Make a loop with the chaining string a few inches out of the lark's head, and place it in front of this new set of warps, then feed another loop behind the warps and up through the first loop. Pull this link of the chain tight, and the sets are nicely segregated.

Wind the warp sets for all the remaining cards (only a few are shown for simplicity), chaining round each set as it is completed. Tie approximately three keeper cords very tightly round all the warps at even intervals. Cut the warps at both ends, just inside the pegs.

Lay the warp on a table as shown, and pile the cards face up in order, with card 1 on top. The numbering and lettering of the cards is the same as already described for the previous weave, in Diagram 42 (page 89). Here, only one side needs lettering, and that side is on top when the card is face up. Lay a ruler over the pattern draft to the left of the squares above card 1 to make reading easier and, following its directions, pass the first set of warps through the appropriate holes, avoiding unnecessary twisting. Thread the warps through each card in the direction indicated by the arrow, holding the card numbered face up, then laying it face down and stacking subsequent cards, also face down, on top of it. As stated already, the arrow indicates the direction the warps pass through the card as they go to the starting knot end. Here, card 1 is threaded downward. When all the cards are threaded, pull the warps through evenly and tie them into a knot. Anchor this knot to something fixed and, holding the warp carefully, gradually release the keepers and coax out any twists and slack in the warp threads. (There shouldn't be any with this process.) Then, pulling on the warp, tie this finished end into a knot. Anchor it onto a second fixed point that pulls the threads taut, and you are ready to weave.

You may want a pencil and paper close by to note the results of your first turns, so that you quickly understand the pattern's tendencies. If this is your very first card weaving, you may wish to use only the four forward, four backward sequence, concentrating on mastering the hand manipulations for swift turns, clear sheds, and even woven edges. See the text at the beginning of the description of two-color card weaving (pages 96 to 97) for pointers on smooth turning and weaving. Sit to the right of your cards and "read" the right side of the cards as you turn.

Turning Sequences to Try. These can be tried on both surfaces, as described on pages 122 to 123.

Four forward, four backward, repeated at least once. Eventually pivot on all four sides, as follows:

4/1,2,3,4/3,2,1,4/1,2,3,4/3,2,1,4 (basic pattern)
3/4,1,2,3/2,1,4,3/4,1,2,3/2,1,4,3
2/3,4,1,2/1,4,3,2/3,4,1,2/1,4,3,2

1/2,3,4,1/4,3,2,1/2,3,4,1/4,3,2,1

Try other pivoted sequences making 3,5,6,7,8, . . . etc., turns in either direction. Don't always necessarily return for the same number of turns when you pivot back; i.e., weave 1, then 2,3,4,1,2 (five forward) then 1,4,3 (three backward), then 4,1,2 (three forward), then 1,4,3,2,1 (five backward to end symmetry).

Rock around each side (see Diagram 47, page 101) to extend different parts of the draft into vertical stripes. Rocking around side 4 produces rocking around side 2 on the reverse. Rocking around 3 gives around 1 on the reverse and you can anticipate the rest for sides 2 and 1. So, only one set has to be woven to see all the possibilities on both faces. The set of four rocking sequences is:

4/3,4/1,4/3,4/1,4/3,4/1,4

3/2,3/4,3/2,3/4,3/2,3/4,3

2/1,2/3,2/1,2/3,2/1,2/3,2

1/4,1/2,1/4,1/2,1/4,1/2,1

Combine extended sequences with pivoted sequences. Look for vertical stripes from the rocking sequences that contrast sharply with the motifs produced in pivoted sequences. (See Illustration 32, right, for an example of this combination.)

Try rearranging cards, as described with the two-color sequence (page 113).

Try the twisting and double-weave processes described with the three-dimensional sampler of the two-color manipulated weave (pages 131 to 133).

Designing Your Own Patterns. A recommended way to work with the threaded-in pattern process is to design your own draft as described on pages 117 to 118 (or use one of these at first) then experiment with different turning sequences at the beginning of your project on allowed-for extra warp length. Choose the turning sequence you like most to weave the remainder of the warp if it was prepared with a specific project in mind. You will soon find that choice is made difficult by the great variety of patterns that start to appear — especially when you turn the weaving over to discover that the two faces are different and equally attractive.

Alan Russell

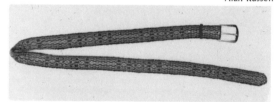

I-32. *Card-woven belt, by Elfleda Russell*

This much-worn man's belt is made of fine pearl cotton. A pivoted turning sequence alternates with an extended turning sequence to weave up the threaded-in pattern, as suggested on pages 121 to 122. The weaving was ended on a point and ends needled in.

On one side, the pattern is crisp and smooth, while on the reverse it is jagged and diffuse. Which you decide to call the front is optional and will depend on what turns up in your experimenting. To find the pattern you prefer, *weave for both sides,* making different turning sequences along the sampler length.

To do this, begin weaving the usual way, reading the side of the cards that is on top. Start with side 4 up and weave one full — four turns forward, four turns backward — sequence plus one repeat, to see whether the smooth or jagged surface is on top. This turning sequence will produce the basic pattern motif on the upper surface.

To weave for the other side, turn the weaving and cards over, so the underneath surface is now on top, and continue weaving, reading the sides of the cards that are now on top. To repeat that motif you just made, but on the new side now, weave the same four turns forward, four turns backward sequence.

Before concluding which side you prefer, try some of the turning sequences listed after the threading process. Sometimes beautiful motifs result unexpectedly on the reverse side of a chance combination of turns.

Four-Harness Patterns Woven with Cards

A Pack of Square Cards Is a Four-Harness Loom, and More! A pack of square cards is equivalent to a four-harness loom. When each card carries only one thread, the cards can be aligned to weave one pattern automatically, then realigned to weave other patterns. Once the pack is strung, you are, in fact, free to weave, by rearranging a single string-up, a great variety of traditional four-harness patterns. (Octagonal cards can be used to weave eight-harness patterns.)

If a narrow strip of weaving is wanted, it can be more convenient to do it with cards than on a loom. If you don't have a multiharness loom, the simple method shown here of translating instructions for on-loom weaving to the threading and turning of cards can permit you to explore on-loom pattern weaving without a loom.

Combining Card Weaving with On-Loom Weaving. The opportunity to weave on-loom patterns with cards is very useful where flaps of card weaving are being incorporated into a piece of on-loom weaving that involves orchestrations of a particular pattern weave. In this case, as they pop out of the surface of the loom weaving, the card-woven flaps have the option to continue the patterns and textures of that on-loom weaving.

Leaving Holes Empty Makes Weft Show. As mentioned already, this card weaving differs from all that previously described, in that some card holes are skipped, causing the weft to appear on the surface wherever a warp thread is missing.

A combination of both warps and wefts now makes up the pattern surface, replacing the four-ply twisted warp face weave of the previous card weaving. There is no twist to the weave when each card carries only one thread.

So the pattern in this kind of card weaving depends on the contrast in color, direction, or quality of thread between the warps and wefts. Controlling the points on the surface where contrasting warp and weft threads appear is the principle worked on here.

Leaving Empty Holes in Threaded-In Pattern Draft. A contrasting weft can be used to produce part of a threaded-in pattern if one set of shaded squares of the pattern draft is left empty rather than being threaded.

Thread the border cards with the same color as the weft chosen to show at these skipped points.

Translating the Threading and Treadling of Four-Harness Patterns into Card Weaving. Referring now to Diagram 59 (facing):

a. The four holes of a square card can represent a set of heddles from each of the four harnesses of a loom; the card itself can be thought of as one dent of the reed. The problem is to get a warp thread into the appropriate harness (hole) for every consecutive dent of the reed (card).

b. The threading draft for the variation of the *pointed twill* or *bird's eye* pattern shown here is similar to a threaded-in pattern draft for card weaving. With a few changes and additions it can be read right onto the cards.

Substitute holes A,B,C,D for harnesses 1,2,3,4 to identify the four horizontal rows of the draft. Number the vertical rows,

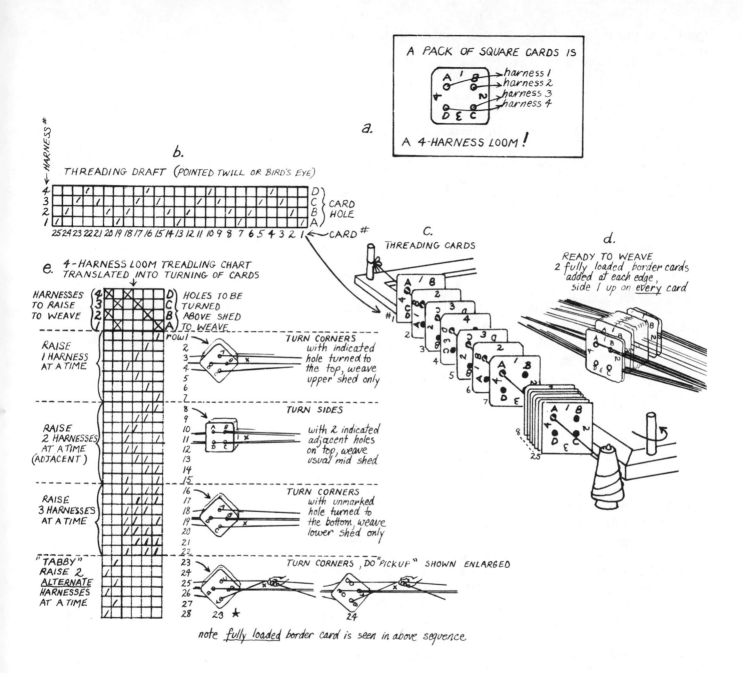

a. A PACK OF SQUARE CARDS IS

harness 1
harness 2
harness 3
harness 4

A 4-HARNESS LOOM!

b. THREADING DRAFT (POINTED TWILL OR BIRD'S EYE)

HARNESS #

4 3 2 1

D C B A } CARD HOLE

25 24 23 22 21 20 19 18 17 16 15 14 13 12 11 10 9 8 7 6 5 4 3 2 1 ← CARD #

c. THREADING CARDS

d. READY TO WEAVE
2 fully loaded border cards added at each edge, side 1 up on every card

e. 4-HARNESS LOOM TREADLING CHART TRANSLATED INTO TURNING OF CARDS

HARNESSES TO RAISE TO WEAVE (4 3 2 1) D C B A HOLES TO BE TURNED ABOVE SHED TO WEAVE

RAISE 1 HARNESS AT A TIME — row 1 2 3 4 5 6 7

TURN CORNERS with indicated hole turned to the top, weave upper shed only

RAISE 2 HARNESSES AT A TIME (ADJACENT) — 8 9 10 11 12 13 14 15

TURN SIDES with 2 indicated adjacent holes on top, weave usual mid shed

RAISE 3 HARNESSES AT A TIME — 16 17 18 19 20 21 22

TURN CORNERS with unmarked hole turned to the bottom, weave lower shed only

"TABBY" RAISE 2 ALTERNATE HARNESSES AT A TIME — 23 24 25 26 27 28

TURN CORNERS, DO "PICKUP" SHOWN ENLARGED

23 ★   24

note _fully loaded_ border card is seen in above sequence

D-59. Translating the threading and treadling of four-harness patterns into cards starting at the right, to represent the number of the card in the pack.

Each square marked in the draft now means that a warp thread must be threaded through only that particular hole of each card.

c. Stack the cards from the bottom up, turning each card so that the hole indicated by the draft to carry a thread is at the top left corner.

Note that any pattern threading repeats a certain sequence involving so many threads. Your pack of pattern cards should be some multiple of the repeat. Four repeats of this pattern require twenty-five cards.

Pass the single warp thread through the top left hole of all the pack at once, tie the end to a peg or equivalent, and wind the warp off in either manner shown for the two-color threading in Diagram 43 (page 91). Since there is no twist with only one thread per card, threading direction has no effect.

d. Two fully loaded border cards are later added at each edge to help prevent the pattern cards from turning accidentally out of alignment, which they tend to do when carrying only one warp if fully loaded border cards are not present. Stretch the cards taut, adjust the pattern cards till all have side 1 on top, and you are ready to start weaving.

e. The loom treadling chart is easily translated to the turning of cards, when you again substitute holes A,B,C,D for harnesses 1,2,3,4. The Xs at the top of the chart indicate which harnesses (now holes) are raised to be above the shed in each row of weaving, marked in the graph below.

Row 1 shows that harness 1 should be raised, so that means hole A is turned up, and as described below, you weave under its top shed only. Row 2 says turn hole B up, row 3 hole C up, and row 4, hole D. Rows 1 to 7 can be repeated to weave a diamond pattern dominated by the weft.

At row 8, a similar sequence starts that indicates two harnesses, hence holes, should be raised above the shed when you weave. That is followed by three harnesses (holes) being raised. The more holes that are raised, the more the warp will dominate the weft in the surface of the weave.

Here are methods of turning and weaving cards to duplicate the raising of different harness combinations:

1. To raise one harness at a time, turn to weave the appro-

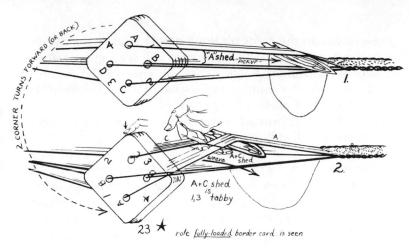

D-60. *Pickup method of weaving the two tabby sheds in four-harness patterns*

The text describes this process in detail (pages 124 to 128).

priate corner as in the double weave process (page 136), weaving only the *upper* shed in this case.

2. To raise two adjacent harnesses at a time, turn the sides, weaving the middle shed as usual, with the two indicated holes on top.

3. To raise three harnesses, turn corners again, this time weaving only the lower shed. Turn the unmarked hole (or one harness to remain down) to the bottom, to simplify thinking.

4. To weave tabby (basic plain weave showing warp and weft equally on surface) requires lifting two alternate threads before weaving, which requires in card weaving a pickup technique. We must lift holes A and C together for the 1,3 tabby, and holes B and D together for the 2,4 tabby.

To weave the 1,3 tabby, turn the A corner up as shown in Diagram 60 (above), slipping the shuttle into the top shed and pushing it back against the weaving. Don't weave this shed yet, just leave the shuttle sitting in it as shown at 1.

Make two corner turns forward or backward to put corner C on top. (Note: since the pattern cards develop no twist, the decision to turn either forward or back will depend on the twist building up in the border cards.)

Slip the first finger of your right hand into the top shed, under the C threads, and slide it halfway back from the weaving to meet the shuttle, which is now brought forward to that point.

Press down on the cards till the B and D threads clearly sink below the A and C threads. As soon as you see the separation, slip your second index finger under the cross of the A and C threads, remove the shuttle, and weave it across between the A,C and the B,D threads, as suggested at 2.

Follow the same process to weave the 2,4 tabby by picking up the B shed and adding it into the D shed.

Altering the Density of the Warps. The cards themselves act as the reed of a loom to set the space between the warps. Since the cards are thin, the spacing is dense and the warps are very close together. It can be desirable, when medium-weight warps such as three-ply rug yarn are used, to open up the spacing and allow the weft to show more in the pattern. If this is wanted, either make cards from a heavier cardboard, such as Bainbridge mounting board, or temporarily tape or permanently glue two or three of these thinner cards together, as shown in Diagram 61 (right).

Interesting subtleties can be made to occur in the weave by varying the weight of the cards across the pack. Correlating a symmetrical threading with a symmetrical change in card weight could produce interesting optical effects in the pattern.

An Alternate Threading Method. If the cards are going to be realigned several times to weave various loom patterns, the following method of threading and aligning can be easier to keep track of when changes are made. First, fill only hole A of each card, then arrange the cards in the pack so that the numbered sides are turned to the top to correspond to the sequence of harnesses indicated for threading in the pattern draft.

Note that in the sampler threading in Diagram 62 (facing), every card carries a thread in hole A, and the top sides line up in this order: 1,2,3,4,1,4,3,2, repeat. They are easily re-aligned to weave, say, honeycomb, by putting the sides in the order 1,2,1,2,1,2,3,4,3,4,3,4, repeat, and translating the tread-ling sequence called for by this pattern.

Adjustments can be made to the number of threads included in each section of the repeated draft sequence to center the alignment of a new pattern within a pack of cards that may not be an exact multiple of that new pattern.

Description of the Bird's Eye Sampler. See Illustration 33

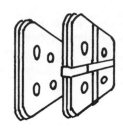

D-61. *Altering density of warp*

Warps can be spaced wider apart for four-harness loom pattern weaves by taping or gluing three cards together.

Alan Russell

I-33. *A four-harness pattern sampler (bird's eye variation)*

Diagram 62 (facing) presents the pattern draft and list of turning variations that were used in this sampler.

128

BIRD'S EYE VARIATION (SAMPLER)

1.

																							D
																							C
																							B
																							A

1 2 3 4 1 4 3 2 1 2 3 4 1 4 3 2 1 2 3 4 1 4 3 2 1
25 PATTERN CARDS

2. Weave sides: 3 4 1 2 3 2 1 4 3 4 1 2 3 2 1 4 3
   start 4 for. 4 back 4 for. 4 back

3. Weave sides: 3 4 1 2 3 2 1 4 3 2 1 4 3 4 1 2 3 4 1 2 3 2 1 4 3
   start 4 for 8 back 8 for. 4 back

4. Weave corners: A C A C ..... top shed only ⎫
5. Weave corners: B D B D ..... " " " ⎪ variations
6. Weave sides: 1 3 1 3 ...... ⎬ of
7. Weave sides: 2 4 2 4 ..... ⎭ "weaving opposites"

8. Using any of above sequences, weave corners, weaving only <u>bottom</u> shed.

9. Continuing sequence of 8, weave corners and sides, weaving alternately <u>bottom</u> shed of corner and middle shed of side.

10. Continuing... weave sides only

11. Continuing...weave corners and sides alternately, weaving only middle and <u>upper</u> sheds.

12. Weave corners, weaving only <u>upper</u> shed.

13. Extend parts of the pattern - see accompanying text.

0-62. Threading draft and turning
equences for bird's eye sampler

lustration 33 (facing) pictures the sampler
voven with this draft and these turning
equences, which are explained in detail in
he text (pages 130 to 131).

(page 128). This sampler was threaded with the draft in Diagram 62 (page 129) and follows the turning sequence listed below it, which is explained in a moment. Warp is a white three-ply rug yarn, weft and border cards are the same yarn in black.

Notice the changing balance between dark weft and light warp, as one then the other dominates the surface, depending on how many holes are above the shed woven.

A white weft was used near the top. The pattern in that section depends entirely on the contrasting direction of the vertical warp threads raised to be above the shed and the horizontal lines of the weft.

The evenly balanced diamond pattern in the center is the four forward, four backward turning of the sides, putting two holes above the shed. The checks are weaving on opposites. Following are instructions for each type of turn.

An Explanation of the Turning and Weaving Processes Listed with the Bird's Eye Sampler Draft in Diagram 62. These are some different methods of weaving that explore the variety available with this draft. They could be applied to other four-harness drafts, or even to the two previously discussed types of pattern threadings.

Numbers 2 through 7 suggest basic turning sequences. Numbers 8 through 12 suggest five different weaving methods to apply to these sequences to produce different proportions of warp to weft on the surface.

In Numbers 9 and 11 you weave side, corner, side, corner, following any sequence 2 through 7. If you choose sequence 2, and weave as directed at 9, weave:

row 1 — side 1
row 2 — corner B (lower shed only)
row 3 — side 2
row 4 — corner C (lower shed only)
row 5 — side 3
row 6 — corner D (lower shed only), etc.

You actually weave an extra "shadow" row between each turn of the sides, weaving the lower shed of each corner as you come to it naturally.

I-34. *Three-dimensional sampler made with two-color manipulated weave*

Twisting some cards over, weaving corners to produce two layers, and allowing a thick weft to pop out from the surface are the methods that create the three-dimensional card weaving variations pictured here. The sampler is hung upside down and backward from the direction in which it was woven and is explained.

Richard Harper

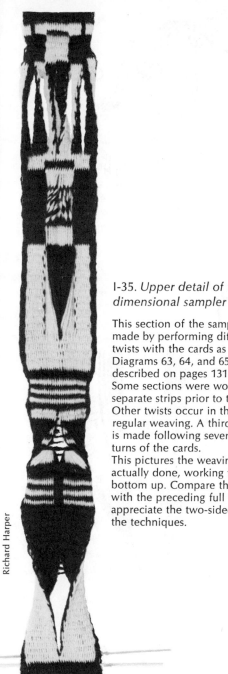

I-35. *Upper detail of three-dimensional sampler*

This section of the sampler was made by performing different twists with the cards as pictured in Diagrams 63, 64, and 65 and described on pages 131 to 136. Some sections were woven into separate strips prior to twisting. Other twists occur in the midst of regular weaving. A third variation is made following several unwoven turns of the cards.

This pictures the weaving as it was actually done, working from the bottom up. Compare this photo with the preceding full view to appreciate the two-sided nature of the techniques.

In 11, you follow the same procedure, weaving only the upper shed of each corner turn.

In number 13, a second shuttle, carrying thin white yarn, is needed along with the black weft shuttle. The white shuttle weaves each of the two types of tabby rows alternately between the repeated weaving of any side or corner with the black weft.

For example:

row 1 — weave side 1 with black

row 2 — weave 1,3 tabby with white

row 3 — weave side 1 with black

row 4 — weave 2,4 tabby with white

repeat 1 through 4

Replace side 1 with any other side or corner to create different vertical stripe patterns. Sustain different sides in any sequence in which you want to create still further variety.

Finally, try weaving as "drawn in," which means following the threading draft, right to left, in turning your cards. Consider the numbers along the bottom as referring to the numbered sides of the cards. Beginning at the right, weave sides 1,2,3,4, 1,4,3,2, repeat. This produces the basic bird's eye pattern of a diamond with a spot in the center that has an even balance of warp and weft on the surface. Keep the pattern but alter the proportions of warp to weft by reading the marked squares right to left; i.e., weave only the top shed of corners *a,b,c,d,a,d,* etc., to the end of the sequence for less warp on the surface; also try weaving the bottom shed only of this same sequence for *more* warp on the surface.

Three-Dimensional Card Weaving

The three-dimensional manipulations described now can be made with any threading of the cards. However, their structure is clearest when made with the two-color threading, so that is how they are presented here. Illustration 34 (facing) pictures the three-dimensional sampler that is explained in this section on three-dimensional card weaving.

The manipulations that cause card weaving to become three-dimensional are all very simple and natural to this weaving

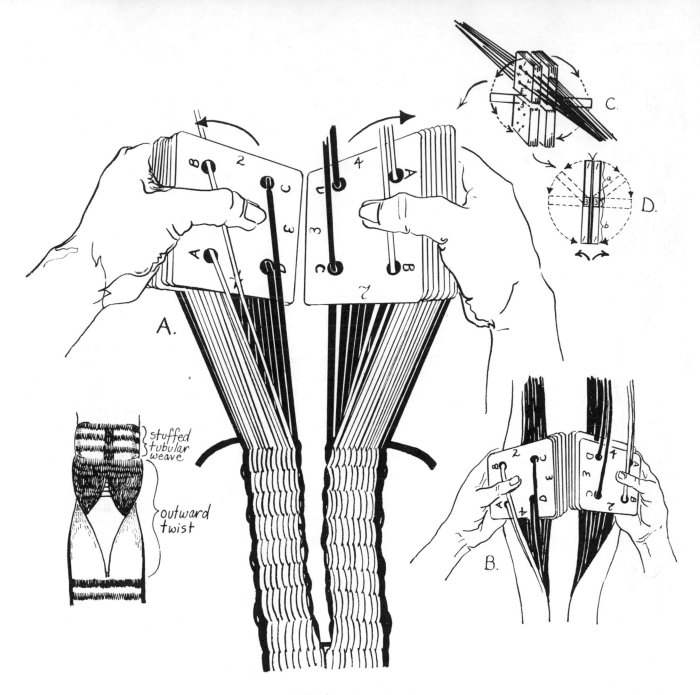

D-63. *The outward twist*

This pictures the split and twist of the pack that produced the lower section of Illustration 35 (page 131), sketched lower left here.

process. They are based on twisting some cards over, turning cards as diamonds to weave their corners and produce two layers of weaving rather than one, and allowing thick novelty materials to protrude from the surface.

The dynamic surfaces of three-dimensional card weaving read out strong enough to suggest the possibility of an interesting power play when they combine with boldly shaped, free-hanging, off-loom techniques. A method of combining follows this description of three-dimensional card weaving (page 140).

The Outward Twist. See Diagram 63 (facing). This explains the first twist of the sampler, seen at the bottom of Illustration 35 (page 131), which is sketched to the left here.

Begin by dividing the pack in the center and weaving the two halves separately. Here, rocking around side 1 was the weaving sequence used to build the strips for about five inches. End with side 1 on top.

Then grasp each pack as pictured at A and pull the thumbs out and down. This brings side 3 up through the center, as pictured at B. The two center cards are now at the edges of the pack; the border cards are now in the center.

The drawing at C shows the starting and finishing position of the cards, with side 1 going from top to bottom.

D diagrams the end view of the cards doing an outward twist.

After completing the twist, weave across the whole pack, continuing the rock around the solid side sequence, now rocking around side 3 to sustain the dark that has come to the top. Continue a few rows after the weaving fills in at the center.

You will find that the twist is keeping this straight part of the weaving from lying flat. A short section of tightly stuffed tubular weave can follow the twist to resist its pull and bring the work flat again.

A description of the tubular weave follows the other types of twists.

The Inward Twist. See Diagram 64 (left). Rock around side 3 for a few rows of regular weaving following the closing of the stuffed tube a. Then, after weaving side 3, bring up and weave side 1, not weaving the mixed side in between for a sudden change (this is optional). Split the pack in the center,

D-64. *The inward twist*

Made without weaving first.

separate the cards slightly, and push the tops down through the center, so they end up at the bottom.

The solid dark border cards now return to the edges of the pack. To lengthen the dark floating warps that come to the top with the twist, the weft continues across the whole pack for six rows that alternately weave sides 1 and 2 only. Long white floats result on the other side. Sandwiched between these floats the weaving produces black and white horizontal stripes.

When the weaving closes in the center, side 1 is brought to the top and sustained briefly before making another stuffed tube.

This twist was made without weaving the split sections first. With any twist there exists the option to weave or not to weave, before making the twist.

Variations on Inward and Outward Twists. At a of Diagram 65 (right), the whole pack sustains light on top for a short distance. Following the weaving of side 1, the pack is divided into three.

The edge packs are woven separately for eight inches, then before side 1 is woven, the center pack, with side 1 still on top, is split in the center, the two halves then making an outward twist. The weft crosses the whole pack, weaving shed 1 on the side packs, shed 3 on the center pack. Two turns are made to change colors, then those colors are sustained for a short length.

To start *b*, the side packs are woven separately again for a few inches, keeping the dark on top. Before weaving side 3 on them, the center pack is turned many times in one direction, till enough twists accumulate to ply the warps tightly for the length woven at the sides, taking care to stop with side 1 up. This center pack is then split in the center and makes an inward twist, bringing side 3 to the top. The weft crosses shed 3 of the whole pack, then two turns are made with the center pack to make another sudden color change before weaving.

Weaving continues as for sustained checks for a short distance, ending weaving side 3 on the side packs, side 1 on the center pack.

Those three packs are then each divided in half, and all six woven separately, sustaining for about eight inches the colors set at their start. (Dark on the sides, light on the center.) They all stop after weaving a solid side.

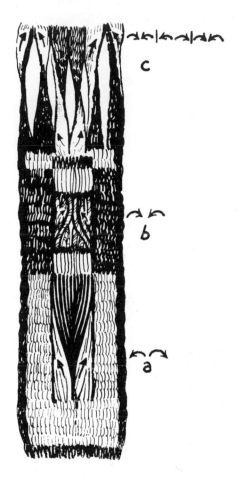

D-65. *Variations of inward and outward twists*

The arrows show the twist directions of the various splits of the pack, seen in the upper part of Illustration 35 (page 131).

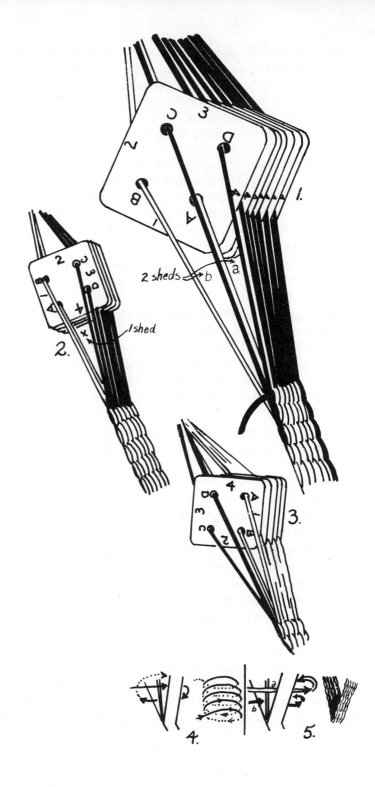

D-66. *Weaving corners for double weave*

The two outside pairs then make an inward twist and the center pair makes an outward twist to produce the twists at c. The weaving continues across the whole pack, the rocking sequence sustaining the color changes made with the twists.

A stuffed tube follows the last set of twists, but isn't needed between the others to keep them flat.

Double Weave: Stuffed Tubes and Arched Flaps Made by Weaving Corners. The principle of double weave was introduced back in the shaping principles in Chapter III, where one layer of weaving was shown splitting to become two layers (page 64). Diagram 66 (page 135) pictures how double weave is made to occur in card weaving by turning the cards as diamonds in the warps, to make a corner project above the warps, as seen at 1, rather than a whole side as we are used to, and as is pictured at 2.

When you *weave the corners,* two sheds are formed instead of one, each card having a single thread on the upper and lower surfaces, with the remaining two threads running down the center. When corner D is above the warps, corner B projects below, leaving threads A and C in the center. One turn forward brings threads A to the top, and C to the bottom, as shown at 3.

Since sheds *a* and *b* are both woven on each turn, there is the option of using one shuttle in both sheds or separate shuttles in each.

The two drawings above 4 show the spiral motion made when one shuttle is used with each turn. The shuttle enters the upper shed (*a*) from the left, then bends down to enter the lower shed (*b*) from the right before the cards are turned again. With the next turn of the cards, the two-part process is repeated and a tube begins to form. If a tube follows regular one-layered weaving, it can be stuffed after it reaches its full length, then closed by returning to weaving the sides again. Stuffed tubes precede and follow the twists, and are seen again at the top of the sampler (Illustration 34, page 130).

The drawings above 5 suggest that two separate layers result when one shuttle weaves the upper shed (*a*) of each turn, and a different shuttle weaves the lower shed (*b*) of each turn.

To weave either tubes or two layers, alternately rock between any two adjacent corners to weave the upper layer — and the

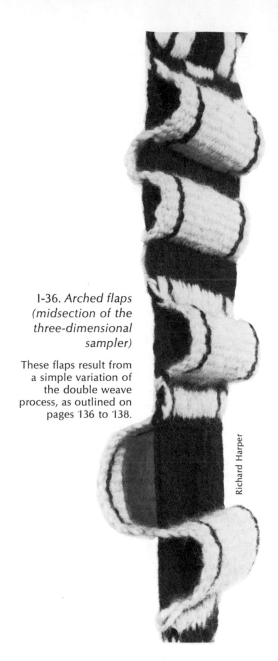

I-36. *Arched flaps (midsection of the three-dimensional sampler)*

These flaps result from a simple variation of the double weave process, as outlined on pages 136 to 138.

Richard Harper

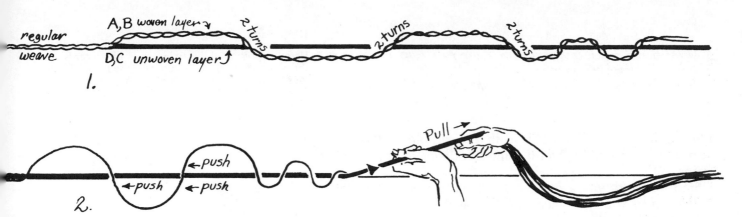

regular weave

A,B woven layer → 2 turns 2 turns 2 turns

D,C unwoven layer ↑

1.

2. ←push ←push ←push

Pull →

D-67. *Making arched flaps*

lower layer is automatically made of the remaining two adjacent corners.

The process of weaving the *arched flaps* in Illustration 36 (facing) is pictured in Diagram 67 (above). Regular one-layered weave immediately precedes the arched section. You start as though to weave two layers, so the first step is to decide which pair of corners is to make up the arched layer. Here, corners A and B are chosen. Weave those corners for approximately two and a half inches. Leave the C and D warps unwoven throughout.

After the A,B length has been woven a short distance on top, two turns forward (don't weave mixed side) makes this light layer plunge below the dark unwoven warps. The light layer is then woven a short distance on this other side of the dark warps (turn the work over so you can see what you are doing) by again weaving alternately the A and B corners.

Eventually return the light threads to the top again with two turns. Stop after weaving a series of six or seven different or similar lengths alternately above and below the unwoven dark warps.

Next, work accumulated twists up to the far end as shown in Diagram 56 (page 115). Then let out the tie holding the beginning end of the weaving taut to let a little slack into the warp. As shown at 2, pull on the dark unwoven warps just following the series of flaps. Push back on the flaps as you do so they are forced to bulge into arches. The idea is to let just enough slack into the warps to allow these arches to rise up as far as their woven lengths will allow.

Work the slack pulled into the dark warps up to the far end

Alignment of sides → {2,1, /1, 2, 3, 4/4, 3, 2, 1, 4, /4, 1, 2, /2, 1, 4, 3, /3, 4

Threading direction → { ↘   ↗   →   ↗   →   ↗

Weaving process → { *copy alignment of sides, reading left to right*
weave sides: 2, 1, 2, 3, 4, 3, ...etc.

D-68. *Random diagonals*

Here is a portion of the arrangement of the cards that wove the irregular texture near the top of Illustration 37. Listed is only one of any pivoted forward-backward turning sequences that can be applied.

and attach a tie to hold it taut to that fixed point. Adjust the tie at the starting end tighter if some slack remains in the light warps.

Start and end with a section of regular weave to trap the arches where you want them. (Note that the dark strips seen running through the arches of the sampler are border cards displaced by the last set of twists.)

Random Diagonals. Below the centrally pivoted diagonal stripes of Illustration 37 (right), the diagonals break into an irregular pattern of what I call *random diagonals*. The title describes a casual, haphazard sequential alignment of the sides that intentionally pivots nonsymmetrically, and at different points, with various forward and backward turning sequences. Try different pivoting rhythms.

Diagram 68 (above) shows a portion of the alignment used here. The threading direction correlates to each ascending and descending section to produce all smooth diagonals.

Curved Stuffed Tubes. Three stuffed tubes were made below the random diagonals. The center tube was made shorter than the others, continuing with the alignment set by the random diagonals. The cards of the side tubes were realigned before being woven to have side 1 on top.

When all three tubes reached their full lengths they were stuffed by pushing cotton batting down with a pencil. The tie holding the finishing end of the warp was let out slightly to allow just enough slack to let the outside tubes be pushed down till their ends lined up with the end of the shorter tube. That tie was then fixed to keep that tension on all the warps, and another tie was added to pull the slack out of the center warps. One wide tube was made next, using all the warps.

Protruding Inlaid Weft. At the bottom of Illustration 37 thick handspun white mohair was laid in with the continuing weft,

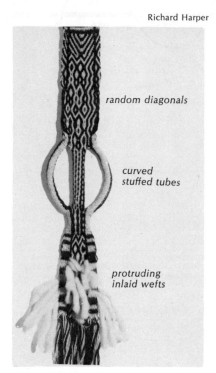

Richard Harper

random diagonals

curved stuffed tubes

protruding inlaid wefts

I-37. *Lower detail of the three-dimensional sampler*

This portion of the three-dimensional sampler is pictured upside down from the direction in which it was actually woven, meaning it developed from the top to the bottom.

Pictured are two ways of laying novelty materials in with the continuous weft. Raw fleece can also be used (see Illustration 29, page 116). Ribbons, raffia, sticks, hanks of working strings can all poke out of the weaving.

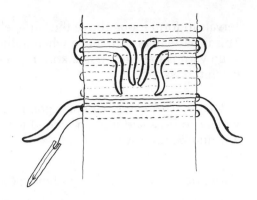

D-70. *A card-woven fringe*

to pop out the sides and upper surface. Diagram 69 (above) pictures the process.

Diagram 70 (left) pictures a *card-woven fringe,* which also uses one constant weft plus inlaid protruding wefts. Doubled lengths of fringe are precut. One tail is laid into one row, the other half is curved over at the top and laid into the next row. Both ends protrude at the bottom to make a very decorative fringe with many household and clothing applications. Edge trims for cushions, drapes, ponchos, wall hangings — these are only some of many possibilities.

D-71. *Altering the texture*

1. After the shuttle has woven across, a knitting needle can pull that weft up between any warps so it forms a raised loop. A tightly handspun weft forms springy loops.
2. Very few cards may be strung, and kept wide apart during weaving to allow the weft to show.

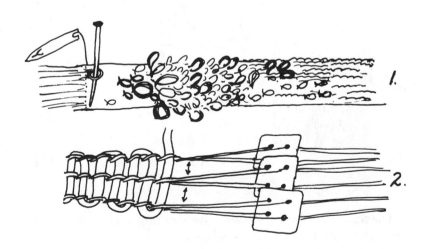

Pulled-Up Loops. The weft can be pulled up out of the top surface of some plain card weaving at irregular or regular intervals to form loops above the surface (Diagram 71, page 139). This is particularly attractive when a thick, tightly twisted hand-spun yarn is the weft. Use a knitting needle or crochet hook to catch the weft.

Inlay into Arched Flaps. Diagram 72 (right) shows that long wefts can be inlaid into an arched flap, to be worked by hand any number of ways.

Card Tricks: Shaping and Combining Card Weaving

All of the tricks that precede and follow now can be worked alone as shown or can occur while this flexible technique is combining with other off-loom techniques.

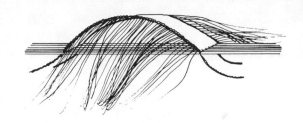

D-72. *Working strings project from an arched flap*

Inlaid working strings can later be shaped down and across the lower unworked layer of warps — using any other off-loom technique.

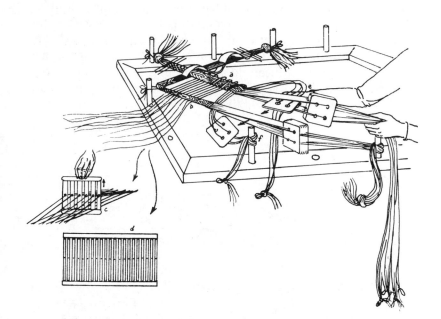

D-73. *Multiple strips of card weaving worked on a pegged frame*

This is the handiest way to shape card weaving and combine it with other off-loom techniques.

Diagram 73 (above) shows how working a combination of several shaped card-woven strips and other off-loom techniques within a pegged frame makes it easy to change direction with the card weaving, and to apply temporary anchors wherever tension is needed at the moment. Bang together your own frame with two-by-threes, making it approximately 26" x 34".

I-38. *Shaped card weaving in progress, by Sheila Myers*

Here are the results of this student's participation in a two-day workshop exploring shaped and combined card weaving.

I-39. Untitled, *by Sheila Myers*

Shaped knotting intertwines with the card weaving to finish the piece shown starting in Illustration 38 (page 141).
Note the hanging solution.

I-40. Girdle *(2' x 8'), by Elfleda Russell*

This piece of linen and handspun alpaca was also worked in a pegged frame. A few strips of card weaving zigzag across repeated wefts.

Drill holes to add pegs as you need them. Reinforce the corners with metal L's for rigidity. If you already have a *warping frame*, which looks similar to this and is used to prepare warps for on-loom weaving, you're all set. If you make this yourself, use it to wind off quickly card warps and working strings.

Point *a* in this diagram shows the top loops of pairs of working strings whose two tails act as two consecutive wefts, then grow out to the left to be wefts a second time at *b*. Their length trapped between the two card strips can be woven or knotted into later and can be adjusted by pulling on the tails to bring the card strips closer together at some point.

The tails of these working strings can then perform any off-loom technique or can be threaded into new cards (filling only two holes and weaving corners), or ends can be threaded into a *Popsicle-stick loom* (*c*), or into a long rigid heddle (*d*), made of fine dowels. Make either yourself, first drilling holes at the center of each stick, then sandwiching their ends between other sticks. Pass working strings alternately through a hole, a space, a hole, a space. Stretch ends taut and make the two weaving sheds by raising the heddle, as shown at *c*. Weave that row, then push the heddle right down and weave back.

Big areas of weaving can be built up quickly this way.

Hang this frame on the wall if you prefer to work vertically and see threads fall, as I do.

Illustration 38 (page 141) shows how far one student worked this process by the end of a two-day workshop. Illustration 39 (facing) pictures the finished piece.

Illustration 40, *Girdle* (facing), presents the piece worked as this process was being invented. Thick white and black handspun alpaca act as repeated wefts. The card warp is fine gray, black and white linen. Building the whole piece, excluding the decorative wrapping, took five hours, which is fast for a fair-sized, off-loom hanging, demonstrating a definite advantage of combining card weaving with the other off-loom techniques.

Expanding and Contracting. Diagram 75 (page 144) pictures a set of four warps that are introduced as one weft (*inlay*) then threaded into two cards, added at the sides at 2 and in the center at 3.

Eliminating cards to narrow work is easily accomplished. Slip cards off and use the released warps as wefts, or continue

2 sheds of cardweaving

D-74. *Inlaid bundles of working strings*

Prepared bundles of working strings can be caught into the building chain or into sheds of card weaving. Wrapped loop-end sticks out one side, tails the other, to be worked later with free-hanging techniques or threaded into a new set of cards.

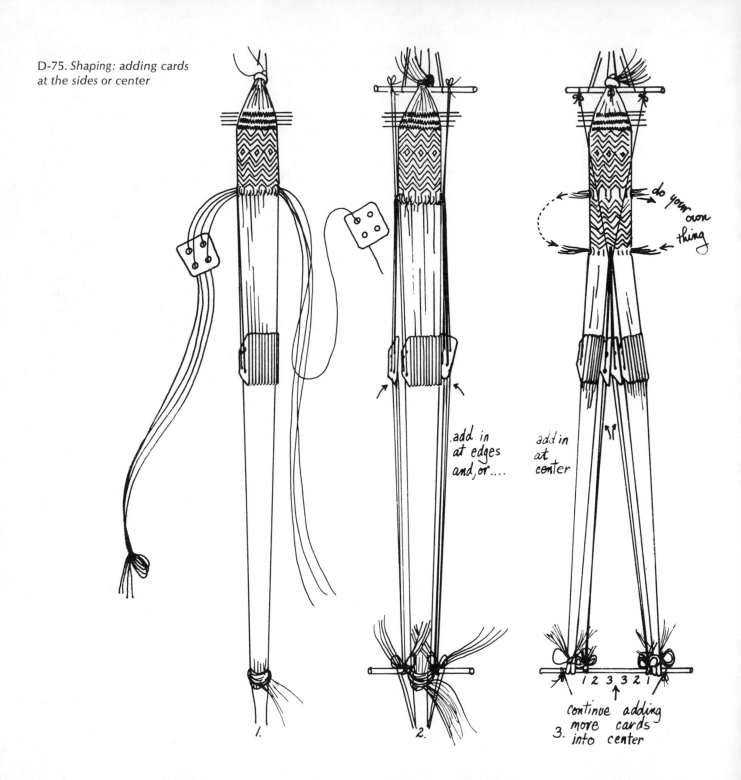

D-75. *Shaping: adding cards at the sides or center*

add in at edges and, or....

add in at center

do your own thing

1 2 3 3 2 1

continue adding more cards into center

1.

2.

3.

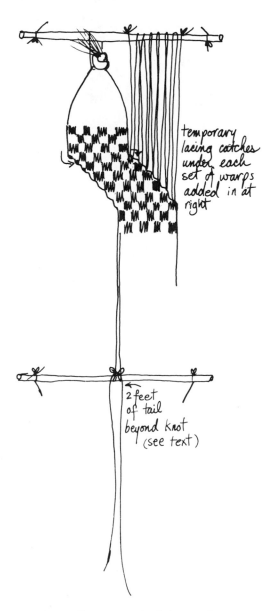

temporary
lacing catches
under each
set of warps
added in at
right

2 feet
of tail
beyond knot
(see text)

D-76. *Shaping to the left or right to move on the diagonal*

working them with other off-loom shaping. Think of releasing warps at the center, the side, or both.

Walking to the Left and Right: Diagonal Shaping. The warps from each single or pair of cards can be tied separately to a stick at the far end of the warp (Diagram 76, left). Individual or small groups of cards are then easily untied to be woven through the pack, then reattached to the stick. Anticipate the warp length that will be eaten up in the weaving, and leave two feet of tails hanging from the tie at the far end stick.

A temporary anchor from the starting end will have to be attached to the warps as they exit from the weaving to pull against the tension applied at the far end. Repeated lacing, as shown in the diagram, is a fast anchoring process.

Branched Card Weaving. Diagram 77 (left) shows how to do this effectively.

String and prepare a pack of thirty-two cards. Divide it into groups of eight, and weave the four groups separately for just a few rows (the same on each). Next, insert a two-foot dowel through an even shed across all the pack, then weave a few rows more on the four separate strips.

Starting at one edge, split each group in half and weave each set of four cards separately for a length of approximately eight inches. When the third set in from the edge is finished, the shuttle can weave across *both* this length and the preceding second length for a few rows to join them together.

Build each following pair and join them till the last unjoined length is finished at the far edge. Build the two outside lengths to the same length as the joined pairs, then insert another rod across an even shed of the whole pack. Again follow the rod with a few rows of weaving on each separate set of joined pairs.

Split the pack into groups of four cards and build separate lengths again (approximately the same length as before). This time, join the first and second pair and all the remaining pairs in the manner just described. No lengths are left unjoined and the joins are staggered.

Continue to alternate between the two types of joins, inserting a two-foot stick in the middle of each join. Extend some joins for long, straight stretches. When the weaving is finished, remove the cards, untie the knots, and spread the work apart on the dowels, as shown to the right.

The design depends on the variety you gave the lengths. Try removing some rods, especially on rows where all lengths are joined. The result is attractive as a room divider or window hanging.

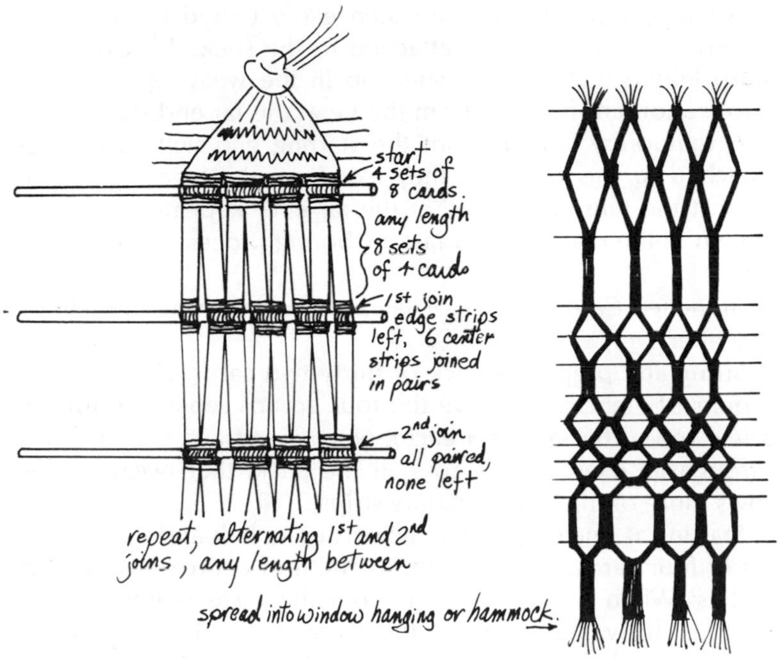

start
4 sets of
8 cards.
any length
8 sets
of 4 cards
1st join
edge strips
left, 6 center
strips joined
in pairs
2nd join
all paired,
none left
repeat, alternating 1st and 2nd
joins, any length between
spread into window hanging or hammock.

D-77. *Branched card weaving*

Branched card weaving can be made without dowels, then be stretched round and laced to a set of rings, as suggested in Diagram 78 (facing). Bundles of working strings and tails of shaped elements can be inlaid into the growing network. Continue to work the long working strings following the general flavor of the off-loom working process.

Weaving Partway Across and Turning a Corner. The shuttle can skip weaving some of the cards, following various systems, to produce different effects.

Diagram 79 (page 148) starts off with a striking shaping method that results from weaving only partway across a series of rows. Point 1 shows card weaving turning a square corner. The process is described and pictured in detail in Diagram 80

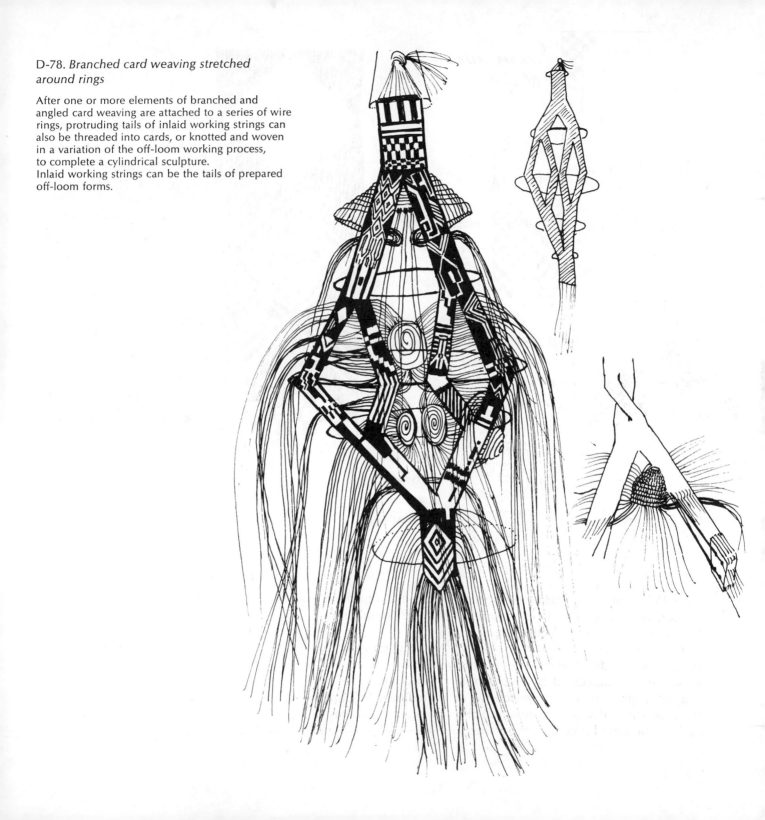

D-78. *Branched card weaving stretched around rings*

After one or more elements of branched and angled card weaving are attached to a series of wire rings, protruding tails of inlaid working strings can also be threaded into cards, or knotted and woven in a variation of the off-loom working process, to complete a cylindrical sculpture.
Inlaid working strings can be the tails of prepared off-loom forms.

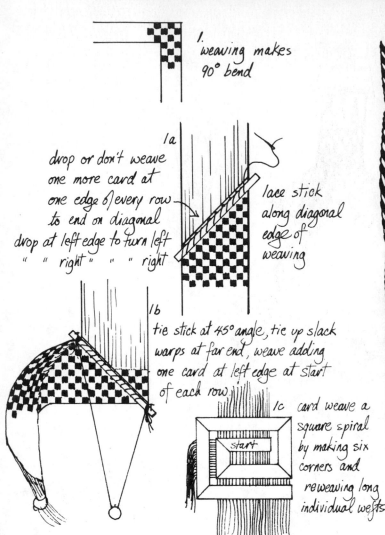

1. *weaving makes 90° bend*

1a *drop or don't weave one more card at one edge of every row to end on diagonal drop at left edge to turn left*
    " " right " " right

    lace stick along diagonal edge of weaving

1b *tie stick at 45° angle, tie up slack warps at far end, weave adding one card at left edge at start of each row.*

1c *card weave a square spiral by making six corners and reweaving long individual wefts*

    start

2c *weaving begins in pyramid when one more card added at both ends of each row after making many twists*

2b *weaving ends in pyramid when one more card left unwoven (dropped) at both ends of each row. (good belt finish)*

2a *work sides separately start each with 2 cards, adding one at inside edge at start of each row, after making enough unwoven turns to tightly twist warps*

D-79. Weaving partway for shaped edges

(page 150). The square card-woven spiral pictured at 1c, which is made with several turns of a corner, could be complete in itself, or the start of something big.

Points 2a, b, and c show other results of weaving partway to form diagonal edges. Such sections of unwoven card warp can be treated as suggested by the *Bedouin Camel Decoration*, Chapter II (page 44) or can be knotted or twined over to allow the techniques of adjacent areas into and across the card weaving in a combined piece.

Alan Russell

I-41. *Sampler of turned corners, by Elfleda Russell*

Reminiscent of *taking a line for a walk* (which was discussed in connection with the *chained skeleton* of the working process, page 15, and with the *free line of double half hitches,* page 41), a card-woven strip can also be made to meander at will. Here, five left turns are followed by one right turn. The arrow indicates the starting point. Note that warps released out of the starting knot act as wefts three times, and walk diagonally through themselves at the top with double twining (page 45). The adjacent starting and finishing lengths are laced together.

Here, in Diagram 80 (page 150), step by step is the process for turning corners. Illustration 41 (left) pictures a sampler demonstrating both turns. These instructions show four cards being dropped at a time, when rug yarn (or equivalent weight) is warp and weft. Drop only one or two cards when finer yarn is used. Sixteen cards are shown in the sequence. More cards require more rows to complete the diagonal. Turn the cards before each row of weaving as usual, making any sequence of turns.

A. row 1: a row weaving to the right across all the cards

    row 2: drop left four cards — push them forward in the warp and don't weave them. Weave to the left, stop after the fifth card in from the left

    row 3: weave back to the right edge

    row 4: drop the next four cards from the left, weave to the left, stopping after the ninth card from left

    row 5: weave back to the right edge

    row 6: drop the next four cards from the left and weave to the left through the remaining four

    row 7: weave back to the right edge, leave the shuttle hanging

B. Lace a dowel or pencil just below the diagonal finish.

C. Attach new anchors at both ends of the dowel, then loop the right one around left and pull it tight. Release the original anchor and tie up these two new ones, pulling as taut as possible. Notice that the warps go slack.

D. Attach a new anchor at the finishing end that pulls the slack out of the left warps. Check whether a second anchor, slightly longer, is required for the center warps.

E. row 1: continue the shuttle, weave left across the right-hand eight cards

    row 2: weave back to the right

    row 3: weave left across twelve cards

    row 4: weave back to the right

    row 5: weave left across sixteen cards

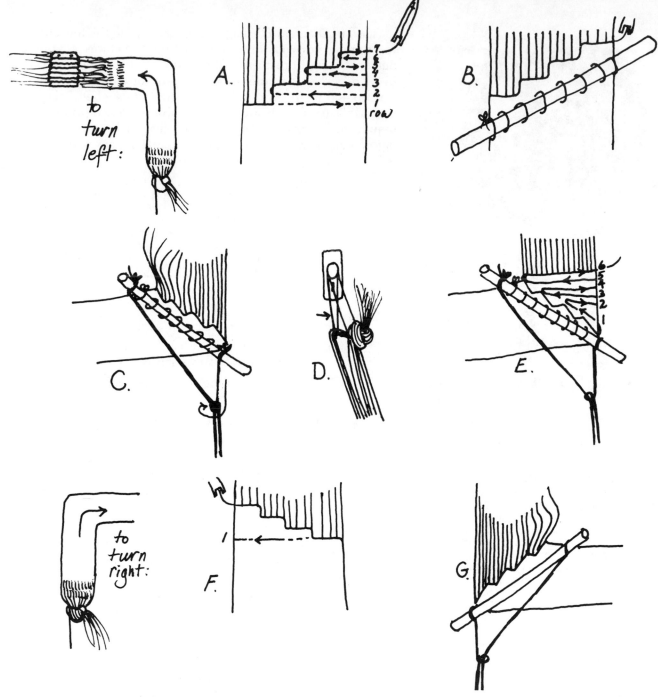

to turn left:

A.

7
6
5
4
3
2
1
row

B.

C.

D.

E.

6
5
4
3
2
1

to turn right:

F.

1

G.

D-80. Turning corners detailed

D-81. *Card-woven tapestry*

As described on page 152, a pack of two to three hundred can be used if portions are turned individually. A shuttle and shed stick work above and below the cards. The pack at 2 is shown narrower for simplicity of presentation. The pieces being joined at 6 could be sections of a rug, the sides of a bag, parts of a poncho, the sides of a cushion, or pieces of a hanging.

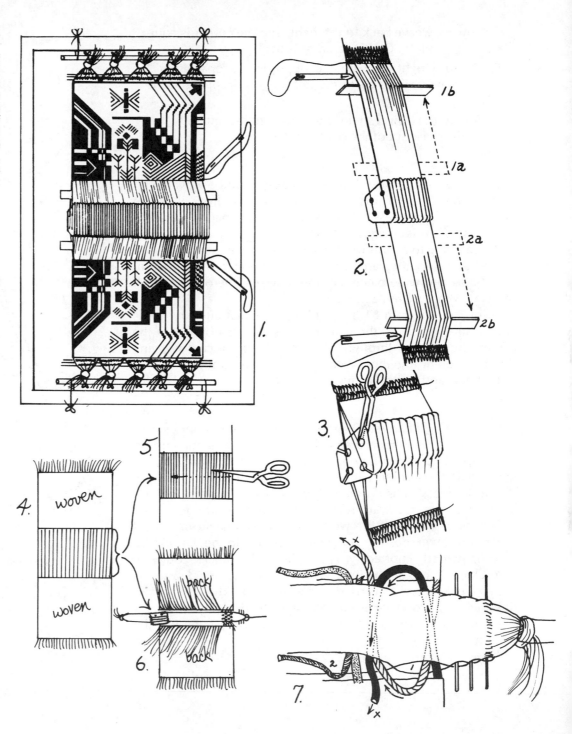

row 6: weave back to the right, and the corner is complete. Continue on as usual

F. To turn right, end on the opposite diagonal. Row 1 weaves across all to the left, begins dropping at the right.

G. Tie up the dowel so it slopes down to the left and takes the slack out of the right-hand warps

Card-Woven Tapestry. A type of tapestry can be woven with a very wide pack of cards, say two or three hundred, once you understand the process of turning parts of the pack separately, as discussed earlier (pages 102 to 104).

When going to all this trouble why not weave the shed above as well as below the cards and get two pieces for the price of one? Short and wide pieces are the only sensible ones to work this way. Work within a frame for ease.

Point 7 of Diagram 81 (page 151) shows that after the cards are cut and removed, the center warps can also be cut in the center, then woven through a horizontal strip of card weaving that joins them together. Weave each tail, or group of two to four, back and forth through a minimum of two sheds for security.

Use of an Armature. Diagram 82 (right) shows how card weaving can be done as a straight strip, then later spread into the shape of a temporary *armature* or rigid support that the weft has looped around at either end of each row of weaving. When the weaving is finished, these sticks are slipped out and the ends of the card warp released, to allow the strip to spread to the looped ends of the weft in whatever straight or curved separations you desire. The weft gaps could be left or be woven, twined, knotted, wrapped later. The sticks could be wire shaped into undulating curves. If a fairly rigid warp — such as jute rope — is carried in the cards, and the weft is, say, one-inch sisal rope, or even wet cane, then a very firm, odd shape could be produced very quickly, which may be just the beginning.

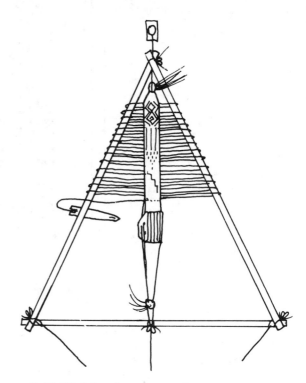

D-82. *Weft hooks over armature*

A straight **strip** of card weaving later spreads apart into the shape of any temporary armature, as described **on this page.**

V

IDEAS AND INSPIRATION

The presentation of the off-loom and card weaving techniques has attempted to demonstrate how they themselves can be an endless source of ideas. Of the works that follow now, some are further examples of ideas growing out of the medium, while others are examples of the medium being used as a means through which ideas are expressed that originated outside of it.

From the examples here, which include building onto found objects, finding inspiration in nature, making functional objects also beautiful, speaking philosophically about the nature of weaving, fibers, one's self, the student will find a variety of avenues to pursue in developing his or her own off-loom ideas.

This section is introduced with a photo of nonweaving to share with the reader a type of experience common to those working in the visual arts. That is the discovery of a relationship between a completed artwork and an experience that long preceded it, a relationship the artist may have been totally unaware of at the time the piece was being worked. Illustration 48 (page 162), château spires, is a photograph taken by myself years before any involvement in weaving, yet would seem to have been taken by someone looking for resemblances to card woven strips and macramé sculpture. Even more surprising to me, the spire at right bears an incredible resemblance to *Om* (page 74), which I discovered only recently upon turning up the long-forgotten photo. A comparison of *Om* and the spire may help convince the reader that ideas don't come magically to a blessed few, nor can you create from a vacuum. Ideas come either directly or indirectly from your experience. A vivid experience is stored away and can surface later as a specific memory, as an abstract form, or as vague qualities one is driven to capture. Broadening, and also intensifying, experience will influence your ability to generate ideas. Strengthen that personal factor, described at the beginning of Chapter I as the fourth essential element of working any medium, by exercising mind and eye. Sketch, photograph, jot a note about anything that catches your attention. Doodle a lot, too. Most of all, struggle to recapture the enthusiasm of childhood, before you knew it all, when your innocence made every encounter fresh, new, exciting, when watching a caterpillar crawl over a rock was as thrilling as seeing a castle in the sky.

Evelyn Roth

This West Coast Canadian artist uses mainly recycled fibers and materials to construct events rather than objects. An exhibition of Roth's *Better Homes and Garments* is actually a series of staged performances, where the total form and meaning of each construction is determined to some extent by persons activating them. This unique use of fiber construction stems from her background in dance and from her personal philosophy, which is described in her statement.

Through my art, I wish to make people more sensitive to themselves, to their bodies, to their environment. I want my art to extend their sensibilities.

I feel the artist should be aware of issues in his community and of the world. Today, the issue is ecology and preservation of our natural resources.

I believe that art galleries serve as a space for artists and public to share experiences. Art galleries should not be storage buildings.

My work falls into two areas:

Sculptural wearables: I have constructed sculptures out of a stretch fabric. These structures allow from one to five dancers to move and make shapes inside the sculptures. They enable the participants to explore new movements, new tensions, new spaces. I have held performances with the sculptural wearables in museums in various countries.

Tactile environments: I have constructed a large room for five people from a collection of over a hundred sweaters, which I dyed, unraveled, and reknit. Another piece, the *Family Sweater,* is also recycled from sweaters and is in part a solution to the energy crisis . . . a family of four can live in their home in the sweater without needing a heating system.

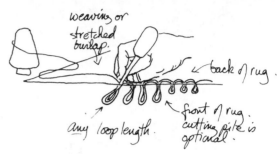

D-83. *Punching a rug*

A punched rug surface provides appealing contrast to card weaving. Appliqué straight on shaped strips of card weaving to burlap stretched on a frame, trace the strips' edges through to the back of the burlap, fill around the strips with pile punched from the back.

Various adjustable punch needles are available that allow you to make different loop lengths. The Columbia Minerva Deluxe Rug Needle contains two needles, one for medium-weight rug yarn and one that takes very thick yarn. The Aladdin Speed Carpet Needle (see Norden Needle Crafts in the Source List) produces three levels of pile extremely fast, but has to be worked with the burlap stretched. With both needles the loops are made continuously so the back should later be lined or coated with a rubber latex, such as is used to make carpets skid proof.

I-42. Africa, *by Lillian Elliott*

Card weaving, whose simple and primitive nature particularly appeals to this artist, is combined with a variety of other off-loom techniques to build a hanging whose title also reflects enjoyment of the primitive. The devices her works hang from are always very unusual.

I-43. *Hanging planter (8" x 8" x 36"), by Elfleda Russell*

Weaving and knotting combine with ceramic forms to build a sculptural planter. Natural flax cord blends with the ash glaze of the pottery, and also allows the piece to hang outside. Cords can work both up and down from under the base of any plant pot to suspend it in the middle of a fiber sculpture.

I-44. Roots *(2′ x 1′), Pacific Northwest Found Objects Series,*
3rd out of 7, by Ann Yang

Knotted and finger-woven yarn and a bell complement and repeat the form
of a tangled root.

I-45. American Primitive *(5'4" x 5"), by Shirley Fink*

A view of a two-sided hanging.
The materials and techniques, as well as the method of working, reflect the rusted metal construction bars that sparked this off-loom piece. Shirley frequents scrap metal junkyards in search of odd forms to build onto with fiber. Parts of an old computer and an old harrow are two other finds that have been transformed with fibers. Following is a statement by the artist on the development of *American Primitive*.

American Primitive is a work initially inspired by the rusted metal construction bars, which also established the weaving approach, the use of a weighted warp with modular groupings of forms (i.e., the wrapped columns and the rya patches of sisal). There is a one-to-one relationship between these elements, a column and a rya section for every space in the bars. The materials, sisal and jute, were also predetermined by the metal, whose surfaces, rusted by natural elements, suggested the materials, which were also natural.

The hanging evolved as a two-sided work when it became clear that the soumak [twined] section when reversed was a satisfying Egyptian knot, not to be wasted against a wall; so the second side was then worked with masses of sisal into pile.

The title became *American Primitive* when the weaver became more and more aware that the repetition of processes was necessary to create large masses, and that this approach is very common in works of primitive art; in this case, the weaver became a primitive American.

I-46. Half Dome *(1½′ x 8′), by Mary Tibbals Ventre*

This piece started from a large, Plexiglas dome, which has heavy jute and yarn crocheted around it, and hung below. Later, holes were drilled in the face of the dome, and fiber tendrils crocheted through, forming an inside-to-outside network that tumbles down the front.

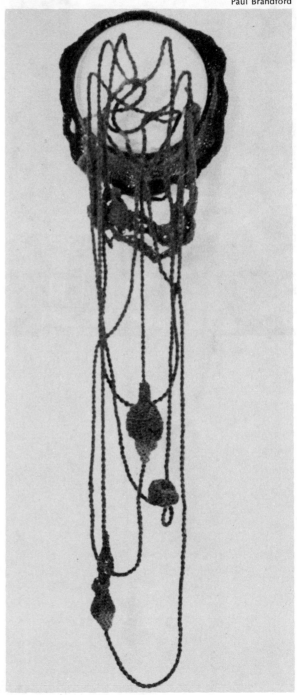

Paul Brandford

I-47. Dome with Braids, *by Mary Tibbals Ventre*

In this second piece from the *Dome* series, we see the crocheted network pop through a smaller transparent dome and fall below, swelling here and there into humorous baubles. The piece could well be the weaver's fantasy of an old grandfather clock, in keeping with a continuing quality about her work that suggests she is haunted by memories of precious old things dug out of the attic.

General comments on her work, by Mary Tibbals Ventre:

> My fiber pieces are the realization of ideas for fiber construction that I first see in my head, ideas that can only be realized in constructions of fibrous elements. The techniques I use — primarily weaving and crochet — are important to me insofar as they serve to build forms, as vehicles for carrying out my ideas.

I-48. *Château spires*

Architectural forms, old and new, can suggest fiber forms. The spires of a French château are amazingly reminiscent of card weaving and shaped macramé and weaving. Note the similarity between the spire at right and the top of *Om,* page 74. The photograph was taken eight years before that weaving was done, four years before the fiber medium was taken up, and never referred to as direct stimulation for a weaving. It's a convincing argument for the fact that strong impressions, though submerged, stay with you and fill out your vocabulary of forms. The individual spires suggest complete sculptures, the cluster suggests the possibility of a grouping of related standing structures. The photograph as a whole, viewed right side up and upside down, conveys still other compositional implications for hangings.

I-49. *A chair*

A twelfth grade art student has revived an old chair by weaving in the contrasting shades of natural jute and sisal cords.

I-50. Boot *(2½' x 1¾'), by Sally Graham*

A discarded boot is transformed into soft sculpture
by a new coat of fabric, beads, macramé, and the addition
of stuffed fabric shapes.
This piece was the result of a class assignment designed
to break down preconceived ideas of what is — and is not —
valid as a starting point for a fiber sculpture idea.
Students were challenged to use any fiber materials and
off-loom techniques to create a relationship between two chance
and unrelated ideas. One idea came from a word drawn
from a hat, the other idea came from an old boot or
shoe selected from a Goodwill grab bag. Here the word
"flying" motivated the transformation of the boot.

Photographs by Elfleda Russe

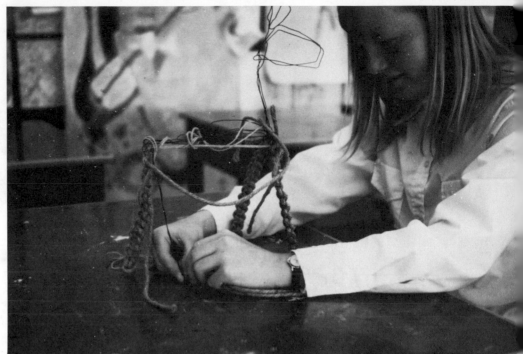

I-51. *Sandy begins her donkey*

Sandy Cooper begins work on a fiber sculpture. This is her response to a project assigned by the author — a visiting teacher — to Mrs. Isabel Dunsmore's eighth grade class at Sir Winston Churchill Secondary School in Vancouver, British Columbia. After learning three macramé knots and finger weaving, each student created a sculpture using flax cord and jute rope and the option of wire as armature. The subject and form remained the choice of each. Sandy chose an animal theme, as did several students, some of whom did portraits of their pets. Other topics ranged from jewelry boxes to crowns, flowers, covered bottles, and abstract sculptures.

I-52. Donkey *(1½' x 2'), by Sandy Cooper*

After a wire and rope outline of the animal was complete, the legs were covered with square knots of heavy jute rope. Working strings of lighter-weight flax were then mounted to the rope line shaping the belly and worked into staggered square knots up both sides to the wire backbone, which they were accumulated along to end in a fluffy tail. Head and neck were formed similarly. Sandy discovered the cylinder shaping principle herself in figuring out how to build the hat. She is seen now weaving in colorful petals of a large wire flower.

164

I-53. Musical Armor, *by Evelyn Roth*

Evelyn models a costume of knit leather and aluminum ribbon that contains an amplifying device that plays six musical notes as the palms of the performer's hands touch the bands across the body.

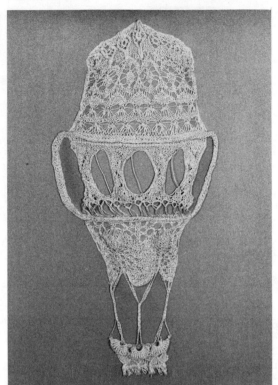

Alan Russell

I-54. Balloon *(3' x 2'), by Mary Anne Brodie*

When a knitting experiment began to resemble a balloon, twining and double half hitches seemed appropriate techniques to form the ribbed basket that hangs below.

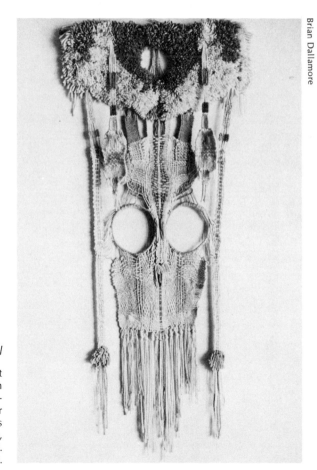

Brian Dallamore

I-55. Mantle *(7' x 3'), by Elfleda Russell*

Hooking and weighted weaving combine in this hanging, somewhat reminiscent of the art of the Northwest coastal Indians, whose design affects anyone who grows up in the area. A photograph of a man-of-war jellyfish, posted on the wall of the weaving studio, was later realized to have been an unconscious influence on the form. Long warps were hooked through the rug canvas when the top shape was made, and wire rings were later attached to some warp ends. Side "arms," hidden by the flaps, are pictured opposite.

I-56. Forest *(2' x 4'), by Karen De Mauro*

Off-loom spirals, started separately, join with warps released at the top of the frame-loom weaving to produce an unusual ending suggestive of tree branches.

Alan Russell

John Wesley

I-57. To an Abraxas Man *(84" x 32" x 7"), by Karen M. Van Derpool*

Dyed sisal, jute, linen and horsehair are twined, crocheted, and wrapped by hand over a welded steel armature. Although the shaping and manipulating were all hand controlled, for convenience and speed during a very small portion of the repetitive twining, some of the warps were tied onto a floor loom to temporarily hold them rigid. Any device could have replaced the loom to hold tense the warps in the initial stages.

I-58. Emanon *(65" x 17" x 5"), by Karen M. Van Derpool*

Natural flax fiber and linen combine in this three-dimensional form (detail, page 47).

Restraint in surface and detail results in the very strong, monolithic forms characteristic of Van Derpool's weaving. Resolving unknowns is a lure that continually propels her work, as described in her following comments.

A technique or material is chosen because of its ability to best produce the desired form . . . in terms of shaping ability, structural strength, textural surface, etc.

Weaving alone is usually not capable of giving total form to my ideas. As a result, the nonloom processes become exceedingly important and must be frequently utilized to develop the fiber statement in its entirety. My fiber forms evolve from concept, more so than from technique; from thoughts and ideas that grow out of personal experience, especially those things which have touched me the deepest. Bringing form to these experiences is, perhaps, my major concern — fiber, for me, seems the most natural outlet.

Construction of the form must, at this point in my work, be a teaching/learning process from start to finish. As a result, there must exist a substantial percentage of technical unknowns for every structure I make. Having these unknowns to confront causes one to constantly make judgments, see new relationships between structure and technique, and solve unforeseen problems. If I can totally envision a piece beforehand in terms of the technical steps leading to the finalized form, I will not produce the piece.

GLOSSARY AND SOURCE LIST

Glossary

ARMATURE A rigid form, often built of wire or wood, that supports the shape of a sculpture that is formed over it.

CARD WEAVING A rapid off-loom method of weaving patterned strips with a pack of cards. Contrasting threads are strung through holes punched near the corner of each card. The cards are usually square, but can be three-sided, six-sided, or eight-sided. The cards are turned forward and backward as weaving proceeds to produce a repeated pattern or ever-changing design.

DOUBLE HALF HITCH Also called clove hitch. A macramé knot usually used to produce a ridge or raised line. The knot combines easily with the other off-loom techniques, where its sturdy ribs can provide structural strength as well as rich surface contrast.

FINGER WEAVING Also called plaiting. Usually a small group of threads is used, and each thread is woven by hand through the others in some sequence to produce a braid or flat strip. Thus, each thread takes a turn acting as a warp then a weft, as opposed to weighted-thread weaving, where the group of off-loom threads are weighted to hang vertically as warps while a separate weft is woven back and forth through them. Since finger weaving sequences can cause work to move on the diagonal, bending and shaping can result when the sequence is changed. Networks of finger-woven strips are often worked together, joining and separating as they angle back and forth, to produce flat or three-dimensional pieces.

HALF KNOT A macramé knot involving four strings where the two outside strings knot continuously over two passive central ones, creating a twisting cord.

INLAY A contrasting area worked into a completed area. For instance, the existing weft in a finished section of weaving can be squeezed into waves or pushed apart to open up holes, and gaps be filled back in with other colors or textures of yarn and any technique.

KNOTTING | Tying off-loom threads into decorative knots. In macramé, the art of decorative knotting, an infinite variety of functional knots can be tied to build contrasting surfaces. However, the basic and most-used macramé knots that in themselves offer great variety are the double half hitch, the square knot, the half knot, and lark's head mounting. Knotting can be used alone or it can be combined with off-loom weaving and twining, where processes are sometimes very similar and where surfaces can be made to blend or contrast as desired.

MACRAMÉ | The art of decorative knotting. See knotting.

MOUNTING THREADS | Attaching off-loom working strings to a rod or cord or armature or found object so work can commence. Variations on the lark's head mounting are most commonly used but other methods are also used if they seem more appropriate where new threads are being introduced in the midst of continuing work to cause expansion or to replace threads that are running out.

OFF-LOOM WEAVING | Methods of interweaving and interlocking threads by hand where a loom is not required. All the off-loom techniques referred to in this book can be termed "multiple-element" techniques, as they each involve working several threads at once. Crocheting, netting, knotless netting, and knitting can each be done with a single thread, so are termed "single-element" off-loom techniques.

ON-LOOM WEAVING | Interweaving or interlocking threads with the aid of a loom. The loom can be any device that holds the warps rigid while a weft is interwoven, ranging from primitive homemade devices such as a piece of cardboard, a frame, a backstrap loom, to large multiharness floor looms and the computerized looms used in the textile industry. Card weaving, though included in this off-loom volume, actually embraces both the off-loom and on-loom categories, as the unjoined nature of the cards within the pack allows their rearrangement and separation, a flexibility characteristic of off-loom threads, whereas the system of passing contrasting threads through different holes and the patterned weave that results from automatic turning of the cards is clearly characteristic of on-loom weaving.

PLAITING | See finger weaving.

SHED | The wedged opening formed between raised and lowered warps through which the weft is passed in a row of weaving. Some method of creating two opposite sheds, that is, raising even-numbered warps in one row, and odd-numbered warps in a second row, allows the weft to pass directly across each of the two repeated rows needed for basic weaving, a far more rapid process than when the weft is darned over and under alternate threads by hand.

SHED STICK | A thin stick similar to a ruler, woven into a group of warps, that can be raised on edge to create a shed, thus allowing the shuttle to pass automatically through every second row of weaving. When a shed stick is used with weighted off-loom threads, the return row is usually darned by hand; when the stick is used in a frame loom, a "heddle rod" or dowel carrying strings looped under the warps depressed by the shed stick is lifted to make the second shed.

SHUTTLE

A device that carries the weft during weaving, that allows the long weft to be wound onto it in such a manner that it unwinds somewhat automatically as its length gets used up.

SQUARE KNOT

A macramé knot involving four threads where the two outside threads knot continuously over two passive central ones to produce a flat cord. A series of square knots can be staggered in alternate rows to produce a coarse-textured area.

TWINING

A group of techniques lying somewhat between weaving and knotting, where a weft either loops back in some manner over each warp it passes, or else twists round a second warp as they move together, in all cases completely covering the warps and producing either patterns, as in the case of the double twisting warps (double twining), or else various surface textures, as in the case of the different looping-back processes.

WARP

A series of threads sometimes held taut and vertical, as in weighted-thread weaving or on-loom weaving, through which a weft is passed back and forth to produce a woven, knotted, or twisted material.

WEFT

Also called woof. A long thread, usually wound onto a shuttle for ease, that usually passes horizontally back and forth through a series of vertical warps to produce a woven, knotted, or twined material.

WEAVING

The over and under interlacing of a weft thread through a series of warp threads. Also see shed, shed stick, shuttle, warp, weft.

Source List

Barnett Woolen Mills
520 South Muskegon Avenue
Milwaukee, Wisconsin 54644

rug yarns

Bartlett Yarns Inc.
Harmony, Maine 04942

variety of yarns

Bead Game
505-B North Fairfax Avenue
Los Angeles, California 90086

variety of beads; catalogue available

Borgs of Lund
Box 1096
Lund
Sweden

variety of yarns, including rya rug yarn; samples available

Briggs and Little
York Mills Harvey Station
New Brunswick
Canada

excellent quality wools; good variety of medium and heavy, naturals and colored

Mr. Doug Chalmers
145 Christie Street
Toronto, Ontario
Canada

Mexican handspun wool

Collins Roving Co.
146 Summer Street
Boston, Massachusetts 02110

magnificient alpaca, mohair, wool, tops, ready to spin or weave in; all natural shades; minimum order: approximately twenty pounds

Columbian Rope Co.
Auburn, New York 13022

assortment of ropes, cords, twines; no catalogue, best to visit

William Condon and Sons Ltd.
65 Queen Street
Charlottetown, Prince Edward Island
Canada

wools, excellent for off-loom and card weaving, 1-, 2-, 3- and 5-ply; samples available

Cooper-Kenworthy Inc.
Attention: Irene Marsten
564 Eddy St., P.O. Box 6032
Providence, Rhode Island 02959

most economical source of variety of yarns, including rug yarn; get together for a large order and visit by appointment

Craft Yarns of Rhode Island
603 Mineral Spring Avenue
Pawtucket, Rhode Island 02860

assortment of yarns; sample cards 25¢ each

Craftsman's Mark Ltd.
36 Shortheath Road
Farnharm, Surrey
England

camel hair, horse hair, wool; minimum order: 1 pound

CUM Handweaving Yarns
Romersgade 5
1362 Copenhagen K
Denmark

yarns include wool, cow hair; sample book available

Curl Brothers Textiles
334 Lauder Avenue
Toronto, 10, Ontario
Canada

variety of yarns, nice novelties; samples $1

Earth Guild
149 Putnam Avenue
Cambridge, Massachusetts 02139

all off-loom, macramé, and card weaving supplies, including yarn, cards, shuttles, beads, belt buckles, rings and books

Frederick J. Fawcett Inc.
129 South Street
Boston, Massachusetts 02111

linens — beautiful range of natural and dyed in various weights, excellent for off-loom, macramé and card weaving, also unspun flax; sample cards available

Fiber Yarn Co.
840 Sixth Avenue
New York, New York 10001

variety of yarns, trims, rattail, raffia, cellophane, chenille, ribbons, braids

The J. E. Fricke Co.
40 North Front Street
Philadelphia, Pennsylvania 19106

ropes, cords, twines, jute; sample card $1

Gellinger Feather Co. 38 West 38th Street New York, New York 10018	*feathers, whole pheasant hides*
J. L. Hammett Co. 10 Hammett Place Braintree, Massachusetts 02184	*all weavers' supplies, including colored carpet; warp good for fine card weaving*
Hill and Sons Ltd. Luncan Ireland	*inexpensive rug yarn*
H. & J. Jones 58 Wood Street Liverpool England	*soft spun cotton, jute and ramie of various plies, and unspun hemp and jute*
Stavros Kouyoumoutzakis, Merchant Kalokenove Avenue, 166 Iraklion Crete Greece	*beautiful natural and colored handspun wool and natural goat hair; inexpensive; samples available on request*
Lily Mills Shelby, North Carolina 28150	*card weaving and various weaving yarns and macramé cords; also cards*
The Loomery Inc. 210 1st Avenue South Seattle, Washington 98104	*thirty-six colors of jute*
The Mannings Creative Crafts R.R. 2 East Berlin, Pennsylvania 17316	*wool and synthetic rug yarns, raw wool and flax, macramé supplies, beads, buckles*
Mayatex P.O. Box 4452 Sunrise Station El Paso, Texas 19914	*heavy handspun Mexican wool*
Mexiskeins Sharon Murfin P.O. Box 1624 Missoula, Montana 59801	*handspun Mexican wool in 80 colors; sample card $1*

Multiple Fabric Co. Ltd. Dudley Hill Bradford 4 England	*white wool, horse hair, camel hair, mohair; minimum order: five pounds*
Norden Needle Crafts P.O. Box 1 Glenview, Illinois 60025	*rug hooking supplies and yarn, frames and burlap; Aladin Speed Carpet Needle — speedy "eggbeater" punch needle*
Northwest Handcraft House 110 West Esplanade North Vancouver, B.C. Canada	*excellent variety of yarns, including handspun and all weavers, knotters, supplies; catalogue 50¢, also crafts books*
Pease Complex Box 75 Chester, Massachusetts 01011	*porcupine quills: a hundred for $1*
The Pendleton Shop Box 233 Sedon, Arizona 85336	*Indian homespun yarns*
Robin and Russ 532 North Adams Street McMenville, Oregon 97128	*variety of yarns; card weaving supplies*
Gabriel Sandperil Co. P.O. Box 992 Providence, Rhode Island 02901	*excellent inexpensive source of macramé cords, variety of strings, ropes*
School Products Co. Inc. 312 East 23rd Street New York, New York 10010	*all weavers' supplies: looms, cards, yarns, triangular and six-sided cards also available; crafts books; get their catalogue*
Jean Simpson's Bead Tree 1614 Ard Elvin Glendale, California 91202	*catalogue; beads, small mirror shapes*
Stanley Woolen Mills Co. Attention: Mr. Ernest H. Pouliut 140 Mendon Street, Route 16 Uxbridge, Massachusetts 01569	*excellent variety of wool, mohair, synthetic yarns, including space-dyed; sample cards $1*
String Thing 6649 Ridgeville Street Pittsburgh, Pennsylvania 15217	*domestic yarn, samples $1; imported yarn, samples $2.50; home-spun, alpaca, linens, wools*

Sutton Yarns
Sutton, Quebec
or 2654 Yonge Street
Toronto, Ontario
Canada

good yarns, include chenille, mohair, cotton, raffia, other novelties; samples available

Tahki Imports Ltd.
Department C
336 West End Avenue
New York, New York 10023

weaving accessories, tops, yarn, including Greek handspun goat hair and wool; samples $1

Tinkler and Co. Inc.
237 Chestnut Street
Philadelphia, Pennsylvania 19106

good variety; macramé cords, dyed jute, cable cord; request samples

Toluka Yarns
145 Christie Street
Box 893
Toronto 174, Ontario
Canada

Mexican yarns, natural and colored; sample cards 50¢

Valley Handweaving
P.O. Box 76
Pinesdale, California 93650

all weavers' supplies, plus handspun yarns, fleece, various yarns

The Yarn Depot
545 Sutter Street
San Francisco, California 94102

variety yarns; sample cards $1.50